The 100 Greatest Beach Vacations

The 100 Greatest Beach Vacations

A Guide for Families, Singles, and Couples

IRENE KORN

A CITADEL PRESS BOOK
Published by Carol Publishing Group

A Citadel Press Book
Published by Carol Publishing Group
Citadel Press is a registered trademark of Carol Communications, Inc.

Editorial, sales and distribution, rights and permissions inquiries should be addressed to Carol Publishing Group, 120 Enterprise Avenue, Secaucus, N.J. 07094.

In Canada: Canadian Manda Group, One Atlantic Avenue, Suite 105, Toronto, Ontario M6K 3E7

Carol Publishing Group books may be purchased in bulk at special discounts for sales promotion, fundraising, or educational purposes. Special editions can be created to specifications. For details, contact Special Sales Department, Carol Publishing Group, 120 Enterprise Avenue Secaucus, N.J. 07094.

Manufactured in the United States of America

10 9 8 7 6 5 4 3 2 1

Library of Congress Cataloging-in-Publication Data

Korn, Irene.
100 greatest beach vacations : a guide for families, singles and couples / Irene Korn.
p. cm.
Includes index.
ISBN 0-8065-1975-4
1. Vacations—Guidebooks. 2. Beaches—Guidebooks. I. Title.
G153.4.K67 1998
910'.2'02—dc 21 97-52289
CIP

Contents

Acknowledgments

They say all roads lead to Rome, but in my world, all roads eventually lead to a beach. Although numerous people were kind enough to point me in the direction of their favorite beaches (sometimes with a little arm-twisting on my part), I'd like to particularly thank those who volunteered their valuable time to share with me insights, suggestions, and tips about their favorites, particularly Julie Barker, Ellen Thomas Covell, Doris Gewertz, Deborah Graze, Christine Kelly, Andrew Kleeman, Kate Buchbinder Korn, Burt Korn, Harry Javer, Sandra Korn Labbee, Susan Lobel, Krista Peterson, Jill Schain, Bolton Winpenny, and Liz Wolfe. Lisa R. Pierce and Susan Wright spent hours discussing their favorites with me and helping me weed out the best (among other things!). And my editor, Jim Ellison, deserves awards for his patience and passion for this book. Despite everyone's help, any errors are, of course, my own.

Very special thanks also to my parents, Kate Buchbinder Korn and Burt Korn, Susan Wright, and Samuel D. Cohen for performing rescue operations at those few moments when I felt like I was drowning in a sea of beaches.

Introduction

Say the word "beach" and everybody immediately envisions his or her own idea of the perfect beach vacation. For some, it's the familiar strip of sand around the corner, easy to get to and comfortable. For others, it's the chance to travel halfway around the world to a remote island where the palm trees and tropical fish are their only companions. Still others associate the beach with glittering casinos and nonstop nightlife, while more intrepid explorers like to combine lazing on the beach with sightseeing excursions. In other words, there is no *one* ideal beach vacation for everyone.

In these pages, you'll find the best of all the different kinds of beach experiences. Start with Part I, which divides beaches into categories according to who's traveling: couples, singles, or families. Chapter 4, "Go Your Own Way: The Best Alternative Beaches," includes a mixture of beaches especially friendly to gay and lesbian travelers, as well as nude and "anything-goes" beaches.

Then check out Part II, which highlights the best beaches according to interests: surfing, scuba diving and snorkeling, ecotourism, sightseeing, glamour, and truly one-of-a-kind experiences, like an island that's home to dragons, floating involuntarily in the salty waters of the Dead Sea, and even an illegal jaunt to the beaches of Cuba.

Some beaches, of course, are almost impossible to categorize because they appeal to many different kinds of people for various reasons. Cancún, for example, is in the singles chapter, but it also attracts a healthy mix of families and couples, as well as those interested in sightseeing and snorkeling. A strip of Rehoboth Beach is set aside for gay men and lesbians, while other parts attract families. In other words—don't limit yourself to what you think are your special interests.

Take some time to look through all the beaches listed here and you might discover vacation ideas that you'd never considered before: lounging on pink sand in Bermuda, diving among the wrecks of World War II fighter planes in the Solomon Islands, hiking miles to get to a secluded crescent of beach in Hawaii, re-creating a desert-island experience on Petit St. Vincent, to name just a few possibilities. And don't forget the beaches in your own backyard: The United States is blessed with great beaches along three coasts.

For each beach listed here, you'll find a general description of its location, whom to contact for more information, and the "high" and "low" seasons. Although the high season is typically what's considered the best time to visit a beach, do realize that's when the crowds will be greatest and prices most expensive. Low season, on the other hand, generally offers better rates and fewer people, but there's always a reason for it—usually that the weather is not at its best then. Although some destinations simply divide into a high and low season, a number of others also have what's called a "shoulder" season—those months that are neither high nor low. Most often, those are the times when the weather isn't quite perfect but still not bad (rain showers for an hour or two in the afternoon, for example). Consider vacationing during those periods for better prices without a lot of people.

Before you actually plan your ideal beach vacation, also take a look at the appendixes at the back of the book, which offer hints on how to choose the best beach for your needs, working with a travel agent, a pre-vacation checklist, and packing advice.

By the way, the best way to read this book is under a bright, hot light, lounging in a comfortable position, with an ice-cold drink in your hand. Now relax...and enter the world of beaches.

Part I

The Right Crowd

1

The Family Plan

The Best Beaches for Families

Hilton Head Island

LOCATION: Barrier island off southeast tip of South Carolina; forty-five-minute drive from Savannah

HIGH SEASON: June–August LOW SEASON: November 15–February

CONTACT: Hilton Head Island Chamber of Commerce, P.O. Box 5647, Hilton Head Island, SC 29938; (800) 523-3373, (803) 785-3673; fax: (803) 785-7110 http://www.hiltonheadisland.org

Perhaps the most striking thing about Hilton Head is the absolute lack of congestion on its beaches. Certainly there are people—some 1.9 million visitors a year—but the barrier island has enough wide beaches spread out over its twelve miles that you just don't see the crowding that occurs on most other U.S. beaches. Plus, Hilton Head's other recreational possibilities help disperse the people. At the resorts, for example, which all front on the beach, guests alternate between the huge pools and the beach proper. When they're not off playing golf or tennis, that is. For an island its size, Hilton Head offers a remarkable number of opportunities for both: forty area PGA championship golf courses and three hundred hard court, clay, and grass tennis courts.

Hilton Head is the largest sea island between New Jersey and Florida, making it one of the most popular seaside resorts on the East Coast, although with a more upscale crowd than many other beaches. Here the Atlantic Ocean is more the blue of the south than the green of the north, lapping up onto well-maintained beaches. Although accommodations range from beachside camping to luxury hotels (with more than six thousand rentable apartments and villas thrown in for good measure), the island boasts more than its fair share of upper-end choices. All plantations and hotels have private beach access, and there are four public beaches as well: Alder Lane, beachfront at Coligny Circle, Driessen Beach, and Folly Field Beach. All have public parking.

Hilton Head is the kind of safe, family-oriented place where parents can feel comfortable letting their children do some exploring on their own. As a family, you can explore numerous natural attractions in the area, including canoeing or kayaking through the coastal marshes, hiking or cycling along some of the fourteen miles of the Pinckney Island National Wildlife Refuge, or motoring along the nature drive that winds through the 26,295-acre Savannah National Wildlife Refuge, formerly a community of rice plantations.

When the sun sets, Hilton Head offers numerous restaurants, although many sport big-city prices. Make sure to sample some of the renowned she-crab soup, uniquely flavored with crab roe.

Nantucket

LOCATION: Thirty miles off Cape Cod, Massachusetts

HIGH SEASON: June–August LOW SEASON: November–April

CONTACT: Nantucket Island Chamber of Commerce,
48 Main Street, Nantucket, MA 02554; (508) 228-1700;
fax: (508) 325-4925
http://www.nantucketchamber.org

Named from a Native American word for "far-away land," Nantucket remains just that: a world unto itself where there are no fast-food outlets, where the gray-shingle cottages look much as they did more than a century ago, where a full one-third of the island is protected by environmental organizations. Anybody who's ever read *Moby-Dick* or seen the movie knows that the island was a whaling port, and the Whaling Museum, a favorite with both kids and adults, is one of fourteen historic buildings open to the public.

The little island (twelve by three miles) has only one real town—Nantucket town—a few blocks from the waterfront where most of the shops and restaurants cluster along twisting cobblestone lanes and brick alleyways. Despite its perfectly preserved historic and wholesome atmosphere, Nantucket maintains an underlying sense of sophistication that shows up in everything from white-walled gourmet take-out shops to rose-covered cottages with Jacuzzis. And, oh yes, in its pricing too—Nantucket isn't cheap. Accommodations center around guest houses and inns, with some rental houses available.

You can get to the island by air or ferry, but think twice about bringing your car with you—it's not necessary to get to most places, the roads are filled with killer traffic during summer high season, and getting a place on a ferry with a car demands reservations well in advance. Most parts of the island are linked by official paved bike paths and dirt roads ideal for mountain bikes and mopeds.

Beaches circle the island and all are free (even parking). The North Shore beaches, facing Nantucket

Sound, with their calm, warm water and easy access, are best for families with small children. An obvious choice is Children's Beach with sand the perfect consistency for sand castles, while Jettie's Beach offers water sports and activities for all ages.

The surf is rougher on the South Shore beaches, and there are fewer facilities. Although they're also popular with families, Surfside Beach and Cisco Beach, with waves big enough for bodysurfing, attract a number of teenagers. Madaket Beach also has a heavy surf and is the farthest west of all the beaches, making it the best spot on the island for watching the sunset.

For dunes and cliffs, 'Sconset Beach is east of Nantucket town, near the quaint little village of Siasconset. The surf is heavy here, bringing in more seaweed than the other beaches attract.

South Padre Island

LOCATION: Southern tip of Texas
HIGH SEASON: March, June–August LOW SEASON: September–February
CONTACT: South Padre Island Visitors Bureau, 600 Padre Boulevard, South Padre Island, TX 78597; (800) 343-2368, (956) 761-6433; fax: (956) 761-3055
http://www.sopadre.com

At the southern tip of Texas and connected to the mainland by the 2.5-mile Queen Isabella Causeway, South Padre Island has only two thousand year-round residents, but the island's numbers more than triple during the summer peak season. Even then, though, the island maintains an outdoorsy, down-home kind of feel. (The only time of year you definitely don't want to bring the family is March, when some one hundred thousand college students turn the town into Party Central during spring break!)

The island is bordered on one side by the warm

waters of the Gulf of Mexico and on the other by the placid Laguna Madre Bay, with the twinkling lights of mainland Texas visible beyond. Many of the area's nineteen hotels, as well as motels and condominium units, front the well-tended beaches, mostly a fine silty sand ideal for sandcastle building.

All told, the island has thirty-four miles of beaches, ranging from the more populated ones in front of the hotels that cluster in town on the southern tip of the island to completely undeveloped beaches north of the main town. Seven miles of those deserted beaches are accessible via Route 100, nicknamed the "Road to Nowhere," which ends rather abruptly at a sand dune. You can continue by driving on the beach, but be forewarned: The local saying is that there are two kinds of people who drive on the beach—those who have gotten stuck and those who will get stuck. A better bet for exploring the pristine beaches is from atop a horse. And if you want to leave the kids behind one day, about five miles past the end of Route 100 is a nude beach.

Consistent Gulf breezes keep sunbathers comfortable and propel parasailers and windsurfers. Anglers can cast their lines into the bay, the Gulf, or take off for deep-sea fishing trips in the Gulf, while the South Padre Island Aquarium offers a risk-free way to feed the sharks. To add an international taste to your vacation, head south of the border to Mexico's Matamoros, only twenty-five miles away, with shopping, dining, and sightseeing possibilities.

Myrtle Beach

LOCATION: Atlantic coast of South Carolina, just south of the North Carolina border

HIGH SEASON: June–August LOW SEASON: November–February

CONTACT: Myrtle Beach Area Chamber of Commerce, 1200 North Oak Street, P.O. Box 2115, Myrtle Beach, SC

29578; (800) 356-3016 (brochures only), (803) 626-7444;
fax: (803) 626-0009
http://www.myrtlebeach-info.com

The sun and fun capital of the Grand Strand—sixty miles of beach communities along the Atlantic coastline of South Carolina—Myrtle Beach offers enough variety to satisfy everyone in the family. For the little ones, there's miniature golf, the antique Herschel-Spillman Merry-Go-Round, Myrtle Waves Water Park, and Wild Water and Wheels. Teens and young adults like to cruise the rowdy Ocean Boulevard and occasionally head off on their own in search of a wet T-shirt or muscle-rippling contest. Adults gravitate to the nearly one hundred area golf courses and two hundred tennis courts, while at night, there's Broadway at the Beach, the only place in the country where you can party at a Hard Rock Cafe, Planet Hollywood, All Star Cafe, and NASCAR Cafe, all in the same complex (not to mention the restaurants, specialty shops, Ripley's Aquarium, and the Palace Theater with live entertainment along the lines of Kenny Rogers and the Radio City Rockettes).

And then there's the beach. Lined with resorts, hotels, motels, and condos (all told, there are fifty-five thousand guest rooms), it ranges from the wide expanses in the north to the more narrow slices near Surfside, where families tend to congregate most often. The Gulf Stream flows about forty miles offshore, keeping the ocean waters that lap on the wide sand beaches warmer than other parts of the Atlantic. The beaches are easily accessible to the public, and, unlike in many seaside towns, parking is usually not a problem.

If Myrtle Beach itself is a little too bustling for your tastes, numerous nearby towns to the north and south offer less crowded beaches, including Crescent Beach, Cherry Grove, Ocean Drive, and Windy Hill—collectively called North Myrtle Beach—where low tide leaves the widest beaches in the area. Also nearby are Pawley's Island, one of the oldest resorts on the Atlantic Ocean, where weathered beach houses rather than modern hotels are still the norm, and Murrells Inlet, a picturesque fishing village renowned for its numerous excellent seafood restaurants.

If you can tear the family from the beach for a while, there are many historic sites right in the area, including tours of antebellum plantations; back-to-nature canoe and kayak trips; Alligator Adventure, featuring exotic wildlife like the Albino American alligator, dwarf crocodiles, and giant snakes; and the Waccatee Zoological Farm, with more than one hundred animals and a petting zoo on its five hundred acres.

Ocean City

LOCATION: Atlantic coast of Maryland, just south of Delaware
HIGH SEASON: June–August LOW SEASON: November–February
CONTACT: Ocean City Chamber of Commerce,
12320 Ocean Gateway, Ocean City, MD 21842; (888) 626-3386, (410) 213-0552; fax: (410) 213-7521
http://www.oceancity.org

Like Atlantic City before its demise and later rebirth as a gaming mecca, the Ocean City boardwalk pulsates with an exuberant family energy, as both kids and adults stroll the three miles of boards, munching cotton candy and funnel cakes, gliding down water slides, crashing into go-karts, and selecting a range of kitsch from the numerous shops to take home as memories.

But that's at night. During the day, the activity centers around the ten miles of powdery white-sand beach, a wide stretch of clean beach long enough to provide whatever atmosphere you're looking for. The southern tip, with its boardwalk, piers, and amusement park, tends to be the most crowded. As the lineup of hotels and condos marches north and gradually transforms into more exclusive condo towers, the crowd thins.

The ocean itself is a dark green, backed in several places by dunes, and less rough than its more northern counterparts, though still strong enough that two one-block beaches, one at the north end and one at the south, are designated for surfing, rotating each day. On the other side of the narrow barrier island, the bay beckons with charter fishing boats, from which fishers cast their lines for flounder, trout, and sea bass, while the bayside fishing piers are rife with those who insist that Maryland's famous blue crabs taste better when you catch them yourself.

If you'd rather leave the catching—and preparing—to others, more than 160 area restaurants serve up seafood fresh from the docks, such as mouth-watering crabcakes, steamed clams, lobsters, oysters on the half-shell, and fresh fish, not to mention any other kind of ethnic or fast food you crave. Visitors and residents willingly line up at boardwalk stands for the aromatic French fries for which the area has also become known.

Restaurants, like the accommodations, come in a variety of price categories, so you can do Ocean City cheap or you can do it expensive. There are more than ninety-five hundred hotel rooms, ranging from cheap motels a few blocks inland to Victorian beachside gems, and another twenty-five thousand condominium units, plus beach houses.

For quick getaways, head to Berlin, Maryland, for antiquing or Assateague Island to catch a glimpse of the famous ponies (see chapter 10 for more information about Assateague Island).

Mississippi Gulf Coast

LOCATION: Coastline of Mississippi
HIGH SEASON: June–October LOW SEASON: December–April

CONTACT: Mississippi Gulf Coast Convention & Visitors Bureau, 135 Courthouse Road, P.O. Box 6128, Gulfport, MS 39506-6128; (888) 467-4853, (601) 896-6699; fax: (601) 896-6796 http://www.gulfcoast.org

If you haven't yet heard of the Mississippi Gulf Coast as a beach vacation, don't worry: You will soon. Already its twenty-six miles of sugar-white sand are making the top of beach surveys, and it's a sure bet there's more to come. Why the sudden jump into the spotlight? Mostly because the casinos that have sprung up there in the past few years are adding a touch of glamorous nightlife to a previously pretty low-key area. Not to worry, though, a family atmosphere is still prevalent and probably will be for some time because these casinos are spread out over an area of several towns, mostly in Biloxi and Gulfport, rather than lining one small stretch as in Atlantic City. The other reason is price—so far, at least, hotels and restaurants are among the least expensive of any major beach spot in the country.

The area already has some twelve thousand guest rooms and by the year 2000, that number could easily reach twenty thousand. Even with the growth, though, hotel rooms are hard to come by in the high season, so reservations are a must. Unlike hotels in many beach areas, most of the new casino hotels are designed like full-scale resorts, complete with golf courses, spa facilities, and children's programs for when mom and dad want to get in some gaming action.

Those other amenities help keep the beaches relatively quiet too. Sure, there are people around, but mostly around the hotels and nothing like the crowds that you see at other beach cities. For a little peace and quiet, just drive away from the hotels along the beaches to see graceful live oaks framing antebellum homes. And to really get away from everything, take a ferry or private or charter boat daytrip over to one of the six barrier islands that lie just offshore, like a strand of pearls that run from the Alabama state line down to the Louisiana border. Not only do they offer pristine beaches and relative solitude, but also some history thrown in for good measure, such as Fort Massachusetts on Ship Island.

Newport Beach

LOCATION: Orange County, California; fifty miles south of Los Angeles
HIGH SEASON: June–August LOW SEASON: November–April
CONTACT: Newport Beach Conference and Visitors Bureau, 3300 West Coast Highway, Newport Beach, CA 92663; (800) 94-COAST, (714) 722-1611; fax (714) 722-1612
http://www.city.newport-beach.ca.us

Unapologetic luxury and spectacular natural beauty combine to give Newport Beach a bit of a split personality. It has the largest small-boat marina in the world (in other words, lots of yachts) and a dizzying array of celebrity mansions. Yet it also sports miles of unspoiled golden sand beaches, hundreds of acres of preserved coastal wetlands, and the Balboa Fun Zone, an institution since 1936 where kids and parents can ride the Ferris wheel and bumper cars, play video games, and snack on the famous Balboa Bar, a chocolate-covered ice cream bar sprinkled with delightful toppings. It's also only fourteen miles from Disneyland, close enough to get there and back for a day without the hassles of the crowds lodging right near the park.

The golden sand of the municipal beach stretches from the Santa Ana River Jetty through the Newport and Balboa piers to the Wedge, one of the best spots in the world for bodysurfers, with parking lots located at both piers. The waves along the whole beach are perfect for bodysurfing but sometimes a bit much for the little ones. For a more tranquil beach setting and waters, consider Bay Avenue between 18th and 19th streets on Balboa Peninsula, where the calm beach is well sheltered from the ocean breezes and lifeguard supervised, or Little Corona Beach, in nearby Corona del Mar, a secluded spot ideal for exploring tidal pools and scuba diving. Families also congregate at Big Corona Beach, a large family beach with fire rings, picnic tables, volleyball courts, snack bar, restrooms, and showers.

In addition to the beaches and Disneyland, family-style entertainment revolves around Balboa Peninsula, site of the Fun Zone and Balboa Pavilion, from where you can embark on a sightseeing boat tour of the harbor, start a parasailing adventure, or head to sea for a day of sportfishing or whale watching. In the evening, the pavilion and its cupola glitter with more than 1,400 shining lights. For a taste of the seafaring life, it's Mariner's Mile, a strip along the West Pacific Coast Highway where the nautical theme extends to shops, galleries, and fine restaurants that front the harbor, while the Upper Newport Bay Ecological Preserve lures bird watchers and nature enthusiasts, as well as those who just want to hike, bike, boat, and fish in the protected habitat.

Many of the larger hotels have beach views but are not exactly beachfront, so check carefully if being right on the beach is important to you; a number of smaller inns and bed-and-breakfasts do front on the beach.

Cape May

LOCATION: Southern tip of New Jersey shore
HIGH SEASON: June–August LOW SEASON: December–March
CONTACT: Chamber of Commerce of Greater Cape May, P.O. Box 556, Cape May City, NJ 08204; (609) 884-5508; fax: (609) 884-2054
http://www.capenet.com/capemay

At the southern tip of New Jersey, Cape May provides a refreshing and charming change from other Jersey beaches. A stroll through Cape May is like going back to a magical, romantic time, away from the troubles of the everyday world. The whole town, in fact, is a National Historic Landmark, with more than six hundred Victorian-era buildings.

If you've ever wanted to stay at a bed-and-breakfast, this would certainly be the place for it (although there are also some fancy hotels and even a number of inexpensive motels). Intricate gingerbread trim accents the preserved houses, most of which have porches where you can wile away the time on old-fashioned wooden rocking chairs and contemplate some colorful stained glass. At night, the whole town is lit with real gas lamps, lending an almost otherworldly quality to this quaint little town.

Cape May was a tourist spot as early as the eighteenth century, attracting visitors from Colonial Philadelphia who wanted to get away from the heat of the city—Cape May is surrounded by both the Atlantic Ocean and the Delaware Bay, making it several degrees cooler in the summer than other nearby sites (plus it means you can watch both the sunrise and the sunset over water). Today tourists come for the same reason and so much more, including dolphin and whaling cruises, some of the best restaurants on the Jersey shore, and historic highlights such as the Cape May Point Lighthouse, which dates from 1859. And make sure to save at least some money for shopping—a number of quaint and eclectic boutiques feature Victoriana ranging from dolls to children's clothes to frames and letter openers, but they're not cheap.

The city's quiet, tree-lined streets and interesting architecture make it particularly suitable for walking. So do the serious parking limitations: If you can find an unmetered spot to park your car, it's best to keep it there as long as possible. The Mid-Atlantic Center for the Arts offers a range of tours, including trolley and walking tours, and the chance to view the interiors of some of the homes.

Cape May's most unusual beach is Sunset Beach, where you can (surprise!) catch a great sunset and also collect "Cape May Diamonds"—quartz pebbles so polished by the Atlantic waves that they really do resemble the real thing.

Space Coast

LOCATION: Atlantic Coast of Central Florida; forty-five minutes from Orlando

HIGH SEASON: June–August LOW SEASON: December–March

CONTACT: Space Coast Office of Tourism,
8810 Astronaut Boulevard, Suite 102, Cape Canaveral, FL 32920;
(800) USA-1969, (407) 868-1126; fax: (407) 868-1139
http://www.space-coast.com

The seventy-two miles of shoreline and beach towns that collectively make up the Space Coast offer families a combination of high-tech adventure and back-to-nature wonders. The area is probably best known as being the site of the NASA Kennedy Space Center complex, a thrill for both adults and kids, with a 6.2-million–pound replica of the space shuttle *Explorer,* IMAX movies, tours of the launch pads, and the new International Space Center Station, which lets you actually watch parts of the space station being built. Right nearby is the U.S. Astronauts Hall of Fame.

On the opposite end of the spectrum is the Canaveral National Seashore, a nature preserve where you can see bald eagles, alligators, and marine turtles. A special treat is from late May through August when more than eight thousand sea turtles come ashore at night to deposit their leathery eggs on the oat-covered dunes. If the kids can stay up until midnight, guided groups can watch from behind the natural camouflage of sea grapes, railroad vines, and sea oxeye daisies along the sand dunes.

There are several beaches for swimming within the park, including Playalinda Beach at the southern end, which is good for both swimming and surfing. (There's also a nude/gay/anything goes, including sex-behind-the-sand-dunes beach, but you don't need to know about that if you're bringing the family, now do you?)

The main beach at Cocoa Beach tends to be the most crowded, but also has the most amenities with snack shops, beach vendors, and so on. A highlight in Cocoa Beach is Ron Jon Surf Shop, a pink and purple castle that's fun to browse even if you're not a surfer. Farther south, between Cocoa Beach and Melbourne, Satellite Beach is good for surfing, while Melbourne Beach is a nice, wide strip for the whole family and Sebastian Inlet, south of Melbourne, offers ocean waters ideal for fishing, swimming, and surfing.

The area is about one hour from the kid-oriented attractions of Orlando, including Walt Disney World and Epcot Center, and Sea World.

Jekyll Island

LOCATION: Barrier island off the southeast coast of Georgia
HIGH SEASON: June–August LOW SEASON: December–March
CONTACT: Jekyll Island Convention and Visitors Bureau,
1 Beachview Drive, Jekyll Island, GA 31527;
(800) 841-6586, (912) 635-4080; fax: (912) 635-4073
http://www.jekyllisland.com

For families who want to combine the beach with other natural pleasures and a bit of history, Jekyll Island, a barrier island off the coast of Georgia, about one hour from Savannah, offers the best of all worlds. In 1886, one hundred of America's wealthiest men—including a

Pulitzer, a Rockefeller, and a Morgan—pooled their money to buy Jekyll Island, where they built elaborate "cottages," formed the elite Jekyll Island Club, and created their own private winter oasis where they could hunt, ride horses, relax, and escape the rest of the world. The island hosted some of the most important people in nineteenth and early twentieth-century America, who collectively were said to possess one-sixth of all the wealth in the world.

Today, you don't need to be a millionaire to escape to the barrier island's ten miles of broad sandy beaches, tours of historic homes, and miles of nature trails. You can even drive across the causeway rather than pull up in your yacht, and rent accommodations in all price ranges rather than build your own mansion.

For a hint of what that world was like, though, you can still stay at the Jekyll Island Club Hotel, a renovated version of the original Victorian club that combines turn-of-the-century charm with modern conveniences and is the focal point of the Jekyll Island Historic District, which encompasses thirty-three of the restored cottages. Walking and trolley tours of the area are available.

The one downside to the hotel is that it's inland, away from the beach. Most of the island's other hotels, motels, and condos front the ten-mile strip of beach, which tends to be livelier, with miniature golf, a water park, boutiques, and restaurants. The waters off the island teem with fish, attracting pelicans. Sleek porpoises propel their way through the waves as well. At night during the summer, giant loggerhead turtles come ashore to lay their eggs.

In addition to the full-service seaside amenities, a full two-thirds of the island is protected land, with more than twenty miles of hiking and biking trails that wind their way past three-hundred-year-old moss-draped oak trees, wide marshlands, fragrant flowers, and tidal creeks. Animal life, while sometimes a little shy, is abundant: deer, possum, rabbits, great blue herons, and more all call the island home.

2

Single Dreams

The Best Beaches for Singles

Dewey Beach

LOCATION: Southern Delaware eastern shore
HIGH SEASON: June–August LOW SEASON: November–March
CONTACT: Rehoboth Beach-Dewey Beach Chamber of Commerce, P.O. Box 216, Rehoboth Beach, DE 19971-0216; (800) 441-1329, (302) 227-2233; fax: (302) 227-8351 http://www.dmv.com/business/rehoboth

A natural sandbar community with the Atlantic Ocean on one side and the Rehoboth Bay on the other, Dewey Beach regularly attracts masses of single people of college age through their mid-twenties. Although they come from all over, there's a definite preponderance from Washington, D.C. (about three hours by car) and Philadelphia (about two hours). It might be an exaggeration to say that *everyone* on the beach is gorgeous with a killer body—but not by much. This is a very attractive crowd.

Dewey Beach straddles both sides of U.S. 1, where most of the restaurants and nightclubs are conveniently located within walking distance of each other so there's no need to worry about a designated driver for the way home. Which is a good thing, not only for safety purposes but also because parking can be a nightmare. If you do find a spot, plan on keeping your car there as long as possible. Two main nightspots are the Rusty Rudder, an outdoor club with dancing and live music on a pier along the bay, and the Waterfront, another outdoor club for dancing. For more diversity, Rehoboth Beach (see Chapter 4) is only a few minutes to the north and accessible by the Jolly Trolley, which runs every thirty minutes if you don't want to drive.

Accommodations are mostly relatively inexpensive motels and rental condos and houses that large groups share, either for a week or for the whole summer. Dewey is the kind of place where you can usually just show up and find someplace to "crash" (if you don't mind a floor instead of a bed), but do use discretion: A reservation is a safer bet—in all senses of the word. In addition to a boisterous singles crowd, Dewey also attracts families, and there can sometimes be a bit of tension between the two factions; it's not unusual to see signs prohibiting noise.

The main ocean beach is separated from the town by a narrow dune and although it's a public beach, there are no restrooms or other facilities. The bay is popular for water sports such as skimboarding, windsurfing, and catamaran sailing as well as swimming, but there are no lifeguards there. Adjacent to Dewey is the Delaware Seashore State Park, a more quiet and remote stretch of beach with public facilities, food concessions, and lifeguards, but not the crowds.

Laguna Beach

LOCATION: Southern California; fifty miles south of Los Angeles
HIGH SEASON: June–August LOW SEASON: November–February

CONTACT: Laguna Beach Visitor's Bureau, 252 Broadway,
P.O. Box 221, Laguna Beach, CA 92652;
(800) 877-1115, (714) 497-9229; fax: (714) 376-0558
http://www.lagunabeachinfo.org

A little Mediterranean village in Southern California, Laguna Beach is an upscale mecca for artists and recreation. But take note: If you're not driving a Mercedes or BMW, you might feel a little inadequate. Laguna has always been high-toned, ever since it was developed as a resort town more than a century ago. Even today, the old-world character of Laguna Beach is preserved in the mansions and quaint bungalows that line the bluffs along a seven-mile scenic coastline, despite annual spring mud slides. Farther inland, seaview homes march strikingly up the lower canyons and hills that tower more than a thousand feet above the ocean.

With many artists and filmmakers in residence since the 1920s, the cultural opportunities of Laguna have long offered the perfect setting to mingle with other people. One favorite is the Festival of Arts, California's oldest and most widely known outdoor art show featuring unique arts and crafts, entertainment, and food, which runs in July and August. Laguna Beach is also home to the oldest fine art museum in California as well as the Laguna Playhouse, a performing arts institution established in 1920.

With some of the country's cleanest air, beaches, and water, Laguna Beach is ideal for year-round outdoor and water sports—surfing, swimming, diving, tennis, golf, fishing, sailing, and biking on the beach. Or you can spend the least amount of effort possible people-watching while hopping from microbrewery to café to coffeehouse.

Staying in Laguna Beach, you can experience the charm and romance of historic Mediterranean-revival-style bed-and-breakfasts or even a restored celebrity's home, such as Bette Davis House, an English Tudor built in 1929 overlooking beautiful Wood's Cove. From cozy seaside inns to full-service hotels, there are rooms with beautiful views of the ocean, the hills of Laguna, or even fragrant bougainvillea-filled walkways.

Daytona Beach

LOCATION: Central east coast of Florida; fifty-three miles from Orlando
HIGH SEASON: December–March LOW SEASON: June–August
CONTACT: Daytona Beach Area Convention and Visitors Bureau, 126 East Orange Avenue, Daytona Beach, FL 32114; (800) 854-1234, (904) 255-0415; fax: (904) 255-5478 http://www.daytonabeach.com

Over two hundred thousand students from around the United States and Canada descend on Daytona Beach every spring to enjoy the reliable sunshine and the hottest clubs around. Most of the young men and women who come for spring break will readily admit they came for the excitement, to meet other people, and to party.

Even if you can't make it for spring-break madness, the mild climate of Daytona Beach has long attracted visitors throughout the year. Nearly eight million people visit Daytona annually, filling the more than sixteen thousand rooms, suites, and apartments. The beach itself is twenty-three miles long and a remarkable five hundred feet wide, formed from a hard-packed white sand that became famous as the site of early automobile speed trials. In 1959, as cars became faster and crowds of spectators grew larger, racing moved to the high-banked 2.5-mile oval track of Daytona International Speedway. The world-famous Daytona 500 kicks off spring festivities every February by attracting a crowd of fans to the town.

Driving on the hard-packed beach sand is still allowed on an eighteen-mile stretch during daytime hours. The sand becomes softer away from the waterline, rising in a gentle slope to sand dunes that can reach as high as twenty-five feet. There is a five dollar charge per vehicle, but that's cheap entertainment since the width of the beach allows room for sunbathers and picnickers to sit on their tailgates and watch the parade of sports utility vehicles and convertibles cruise slowly by.

Floats, umbrellas, beach cruiser bicycles, and motorbikes are available for rent right on the beach, and miles of beachfront vendors provide everything from hot dogs to beach towels and T-shirts from their carts. The Main Street Pier offers a view of the famous boardwalk and amusement park below, and water sports are so popular that championship competitions are held in sailing, surfing, and jet skiing throughout the year.

Surfer's Paradise

LOCATION: Gold Coast, Australia; fifty miles south of Brisbane
HIGH SEASON: October–April LOW SEASON: May–September
CONTACT: Australian Tourist Commission, 2049 Century Park East, Suite 1920, Los Angeles, CA 90067; (800) 333-0262 (for brochures only), (847) 296-4900; fax: (847) 635-3718 http://www.aussie.net.au

With a name like Surfer's Paradise, you'd expect this to be a great place to surf—and it is. But even more than a surfing haven, this star of Australia's Gold Coast is a party town day and night, filled with Americans, Europeans, Japanese, and, oh yes, even a smattering of Australians, each person determined to have more fun than the next.

The heart of the beach action is just off Cahill Avenue: a not-very-pretty stretch of high-rise hotels and condos, fast food joints, tacky souvenir shops, and other tourist traps that line the beach. Not to worry, though, the beautiful bodies on the wide, sandy beach more than make up for any lack of aesthetics in town planning. Because nightlife goes all through the night, days tend to start on the late side. Take a good look around before choosing a spot on the beach to try to estimate where the sun will hit throughout the day—there are actually enough high-rises to cast shadows on quite a bit of the beach.

What to do when the sun goes down? First hit the abundance of restaurants, then move on to the clubs. Although new additions are always popping up, some of the ones that have been around for a while include Cocktails and Dreams, The Party, and Shooter's Bar. Or just head to Orchid Avenue and see which of the many clubs lining the street strikes your fancy. If clubs aren't quite your style, Grundy's Paradise Center is a huge entertainment complex with more than three hundred options, and a few miles south, at Broadbeach, is Jupiter's Casino, with day and night roulette, blackjack, baccarat, and other games of chance as well as shows and nearby shopping. Accommodations run the gamut—lots of hostels catering to the backpack crowd as well as a host of cheap motels and an ever increasing supply of upper-end resorts.

For a quieter change of pace, head south to the beaches at Coolangata, South Port, and Burleigh Heads, with wildlife sanctuaries and outstanding surfing.

Cable Beach

LOCATION: Nassau, The Bahamas; fifty miles off the coast of Florida

HIGH SEASON: November–March LOW SEASON: June–August

CONTACT: Bahamas Tourist Office, 150 East 52nd Street, New York, NY 10022; (800) 4-BAHAMAS, (212) 758-2777; fax: (212) 753-6531

http://www.thebahamas.com

A few years ago, the marketing slogan "It's better in the Bahamas" was almost laughable. It *wasn't* better there—the service and the amenities definitely lagged behind those of other Caribbean islands. But a funny thing happened. The government realized it was losing valuable tourism dollars to other spots and committed millions of dollars to changing both the image and the reality of the country. Now the islands certainly are better than they were before—and better than many other comparable vacation destinations.

Each of the islands (more than seven hundred in all, but only twenty-three are inhabited) has its own distinct flair, with New Providence Island being home to Nassau, the political and cultural capital of the islands, pulsating day and night with the spirit of Goombay and Junkanoo. Although Cable Beach is technically just west of Nassau, it's often considered part of the city (hey, the whole island is frequently called Nassau).

It's easy to see why the locals call Cable Beach "the strip," in honor of the parade of resorts—many all-inclusives—that line the white beach. Some allow children; some don't; many have casinos. SuperClubs Breezes, an all-inclusive, especially caters to the singles crowd, with an above-sixteen age limit, unlimited drinks, theme and beach party nights, and four bars, including a disco. A couple of other discos are right in the beach area, not to mention the discos and clubs of nearby Nassau; some, like Bahamen's Culture Club, draw a more local crowd, while others, like the Zoo, tend to attract more Americans.

Nightlife generally starts with the dining, and even if your hotel package includes meals, do try to get out to at least a few restaurants for traditional Bahamian foods. Look for a "Real Taste of the Bahamas" sign to indicate the restaurant has met government standards for providing quality dining with indigenous food products.

During the day, Cable Beach has a kind of do-it-all, do-nothing atmosphere: You can water-ski, windsurf, sail, play volleyball, take scuba lessons—or just lie on the beach and occasionally dip your toes into the warm turquoise waters. Although some tend to pooh-pooh the diving in the area, they're the ones who haven't been yet. Within a thirty-minute boat ride are shipwrecks (victims of natural disaster as well as intentionally placed artificial reefs), beautiful shallow Bahamian reefs, huge schools of fish, and the famed Lost Blue Hole—more than a hundred feet in diameter with isolated coral heads perching precariously around its edge, each surrounded by its own community of Nassau groupers, sergeant majors, moray eels, and other sea creatures.

Brighton

LOCATION: Sussex, England
HIGH SEASON: June–August LOW SEASON: December–March
CONTACT: British Tourist Authority, 551 Fifth Avenue, Suite 701, New York, NY 10176; (800) 462-2758, (212) 986-2200 http://www.visitbritain.com

Often called "London by the Sea," Brighton is as big, brassy, and boisterous as the Brits get (which happens to be more than their stereotypical image would lead you to think). The whole town has a kind of old Coney Island feel, a faded glamour mixed with a rowdy vitality, its universities and artists adding a touch of the intellectual and the bohemian.

The seven miles of pebbly beach are the daytime meeting spot for university students, Europeans who've come to study English in several schools, English vacationers, and tourists from around the world. There's even a nudist beach at the eastern end where a sign clearly proclaims: "Clothes need not be worn." In addition to soaking up the sun, the beach sports several more active possibilities, ranging from windsurfing and jet skiing to bungee jumping at Brighton Marina and West Pier.

If you want to get away from the main action for a while (and there's lots of it during the summer high season), the Undercliff Walkway follows the beachfront for seven miles from west of Hove to Telscombe Cliffs, while the Volks Railway runs along the top of the beach from the Palace Pier to the Brighton Marina. There's also a lower promenade and a higher promenade, Madeira Drive; the best way to go from one to the other is a ride in the Madeira Lift, which echoes the decoration of the Royal Pavilion, the extravaganza that fun-loving George IV built for himself.

When the sun sets, the frantic nightlife begins in England's highest concentration of restaurants outside of London. Then it's on to the clubs and the pubs, supposedly one for every day of the year, with the greatest concentration in the Hanover area. The Lanes is another lively section, where bars, pubs, and restaurants fight for space with funky boutiques and antique shops in the maze of narrow pedestrian streets. For even more of a carnival-like atmosphere, head to Palace Pier, a beautifully built nineteenth-century amusement center with rides, novelty shops, and food from fish and chips to "candyfloss." A more suburbanized and upscale version, without the amusement park rides, exists at Brighton Marina Village.

Cancún

LOCATION: Southeast coast of Mexico
HIGH SEASON: December–March LOW SEASON: June–August
CONTACT: Mexican Government Tourism Office,
405 Park Avenue, Suite 1401, New York, NY 10022;

(800) 44-MEXICO, (212) 421-6655, (212) 838-2949;
fax: (212) 753-2874
http://mexico-travel.com

Cancún is the largest and most built-up beach resort in all of Mexico. Some say it's tacky and touristy, and in a sense they're right: It *was* custom-built for tourists. Back in the early seventies, it was just a fishing village until a computer told government officials that Cancún would be a great location for the "ideal resort." A couple of decades later, Cancún has some twenty-five thousand hotel rooms and plays host to nearly three million visitors a year.

As long as you pick a hotel on the beach (as opposed to in the city of Cancún, which is actually on the mainland), you almost can't go wrong. Just choose your preference—waterfalls, Mexican thatched roofs, ultra-sleek pyramids? They're all there and considerably less expensive than comparable hotels in the United States. The hotels, shops, restaurants, and clubs all line a fourteen-mile strip of sand that's shaped like the number 7, so it's relatively easy to move from to another, although some are far enough away to require a cab ride.

Cancún has become renowned for its nightlife options, offering something for virtually everyone. Rowdy restaurant/bars are popular, especially Carlos 'n' Charlies and Señor Frogs, both *de rigueur* for those seeking that frat party kind of experience. Discos are also still hot in Cancún, with the most popular ones remaining Christine's, Dady'O, and La Boom. If you'd prefer to watch dancing rather than do it yourself, most hotels feature at least one night a week of local folkloric dancing and singing.

If you do hook up with someone, by far the best-known romantic nightspot is Bogart's in the Hotel Krystal, while many of the other hotels also offer fine dining experiences. For "real" Mexican food, try La

Parrilla and La Habichuela, both downtown and popular with the locals, or Los Almendros, in front of the convention center, for Yucatan specialties.

Ipanema Beach

LOCATION: Rio de Janeiro, Brazil
HIGH SEASON: December–March LOW SEASON: April–November
CONTACT: Brazil Tourist Board, 1050 Edison Street, Suite C, Santa Ynez, CA 93460; (800) 544-5503, (805) 688-2441; fax: (805) 688-1021
http://www.brazilres.com

The girl from Ipanema has changed a bit in these past few decades, but she can still inspire songs. So can the guys. Residents call themselves *Cariocas;* you can just call them beautiful—and tanned, and built, and wearing some of the skimpiest bathing suits you ever saw (they call them "dental floss"). Yes, the Rio of the movies is alive and well: a sensual, sultry, sexy kind of place where anything can happen—at least in the short term. Cariocas don't take themselves too seriously, and you shouldn't either. But do take them, if you can.

During the day, the place to meet them is, of course, the beach. And the two miles of Ipanema, in the southern part of the city, is the crown in Rio's forty-five-mile string of cream-colored beaches. The beach is bordered by Avenida Atlântica, with miles of hotels, restaurants, and bars, and locals refer to the sections of beach by the landmarks on the avenue. Start out in front of the Caesar Park Hotel and take it from there. Swimming and sunning are fun in their own right, but if you really want to meet someone, jump into one of the never-ending games of volleyball, soccer, and "futevolley," a kind of combination of the two where you hit a ball over a net using only your head and feet.

On one side of Ipanema is Leblon, basically just a continuation of the Ipanema action, although the strip of sand is more narrow, while on the other is another familiar name, Copacabana, where some of the city's most upscale hotels line the beach. At night, though, Copacabana hosts a somewhat uneasy mixture of guests from the hotels, patrons of its red light district, and a thriving gay nightlife.

Nightlife in the city starts late, with dinner at around 9 P.M. and the clubs and discos and bars starting to move around midnight. Expect to see daybreak during the weekends. The Baixos (ba-ee-shos) in Ipanema, where popular cafés and bars cluster, are a good starting point, especially Baixo Farme and Baixo Quitéria. Dancing in Rio is as hot as you would expect, with disco, techno, and house alternating with samba, bassa nova, and other local Latin beats.

Negril

LOCATION: Western tip of Jamaica, Caribbean
HIGH SEASON: December–April LOW SEASON: June–August
CONTACT: Jamaica Tourist Board, 3440 Wilshire Boulevard, Suite 1207, Los Angeles, CA 90010; (800) 233-4582, (213) 384-1123; fax: (213) 384-1780
http://www.jamaicatravel.com

Jamaica pioneered the all-inclusive resort concept, and for single adults looking for nonstop hot action day and night, there's no better place than the resorts in Negril. Lining a seven-mile stretch of beaches with white sand so soft you could sink right into it, the resorts offer a nonstop party atmosphere where like-minded souls meet, mingle, and play. In truth, the resorts, most notably Grand Lido and Hedonism II, don't just offer that ambiance, they create and encourage it.

If you're not a group person, think twice about this area; no one will stop you from lounging on the beach with a good book, but there are better places for that kind of quiet activity. If, on the other hand, you like your fun loud, boisterous, and frantic, this is the place for you. Toga parties, island picnics where you play drinking games till you polish off your very own bottle of rum punch, and pajama parties quickly dissolve whatever inhibitions you might have brought with you. So do the Jacuzzis and nude beaches. Most of the resorts offer clothing and clothing-optional beaches, with guest rooms on both sides, though of course you can go back and forth between the two.

While the official party line is to play down the anything-goes atmosphere in recent years, it's still alive and kicking. Where else would a resort bus on its way back from an excursion stop into a little place called Rick's Café where you can pick up baggies of pot and hash brownies on your way in? Can't make it to Rick's? Don't worry—although the resort beaches are private, little boats with goodies for sale do make their way to their waters. Other boats carry the women who can braid your hair, practically a requirement in Jamaica.

Although there are regular hotels in Negril as well, they're not as popular with the partying American crowd, and while no one will actually say that the areas outside of the resorts aren't safe, guests are not really encouraged to venture beyond their borders.

Cabo San Lucas

LOCATION: Baja California, Mexico
HIGH SEASON: June–August OFF SEASON: December–March
CONTACT: Mexican Government Tourism Office,
405 Park Avenue, Suite 1401, New York, NY 10022,
(800) 44-MEXICO, (212) 421-6655; fax: (212) 753-2874
http://mexico-travel.com

It was the rich and famous from California who first discovered they could get away to Cabo San Lucas at the southern tip of Baja California, a strip of land that's politically part of Mexico but separated physically by the Sea of Cortés. In national spirit, it merges American with Mexican for its own unique flair: U.S. dollars are the preferred currency, for example, but the language is Spanish (although most speak at least some English). In temperament, the town somehow walks what would appear to be a fine line between frat party and yachting culture and gets away with it.

Formerly a dusty fishing village, Cabo San Lucas has grown into the nightlife capital of an area called "Los Cabos" (the Capes), which also includes San José del Cabo, a calm and quiet provincial Mexican village, and the twenty-mile coastal strip connecting the two capes, called the Corridor. Most of the megaresorts and upscale hotels line the beaches along the Corridor and in San Lucas, while San José offers an array of less flashy accommodation options.

Most of the bars and clubs center in San Lucas, running the gamut from Rio Grill, which starts its marathon four-hour Happy Hour at 4:00 P.M., to the Giggling Marlin, where unsuspecting guests are strung upside down and photographed on the fish scale (now you can't say you didn't know), to the ubiquitous Hard Rock Cafe and Planet Hollywood. El Squid Roe starts hopping around midnight, and, well, you just have to experience that one for yourself if you dare.

One of the remarkable things about the area is that virtually any beach is beautiful for sunning, although the waters off the beaches on the Pacific side have an undertow so strong you can feel it when you're only in up to your ankles and swimming is extremely dangerous. The sloped, soft sand beach of El Médano is the main beach of San Lucas, but it's on the Pacific side, and although it's busy with jet skis, kayaks, and other toys that go *on* the water, going *in* the water isn't a great idea. Along the Corridor, there are several good beaches for swimming, including the protected coves next to the Twin Dolphin Hotel and at Palma Palmilla.

If you find someone you want to spend some time alone with, there's always Lover's Beach, in a hidden cove that's accessible only by water, with the Pacific Ocean on one side and the Sea of Cortés on the other.

3

Two to Tango

The Best Beaches for Couples

Petit St. Vincent

LOCATION: Part of Saint Vincent and the Grenadines, West Indies, Caribbean

HIGH SEASON: December 22–March 20 LOW SEASON: May–August (Closed September–December 21)

CONTACT: Petit St. Vincent Resort, P.O. Box 12506, Cincinnati, OH 45212; (800) 654-9326, (513) 242-1333; fax: (513) 242-6951

St. Vincent and the Grenadines Tourist Office, 801 Second Avenue, 21st floor, New York, NY 10017; (800) 729-1726, (212) 687-4981; fax: (212) 949-5946

This is definitely one of those islands for couples who really like each other and want to spent a lot of time alone together. Spread out over 113 acres, the entire private island is a resort, with twenty-two cottages and a main building that houses a lounge and restaurant. The large cottages are in beachside, cliffside, and bluffside locations, with varying degrees of privacy—some are fairly close to each other, while others are completely secluded. If the location or degree of privacy of your cottage is really important, talk to the staff when you make your reservations to determine and request the cottage that best suits your needs. Although it won't confirm the exact cottage until late in the game, the resort will try to honor your request if possible.

Completed in 1969, the cottages are built of blue bitch stone and hardwood. Each has a living room, bedroom, bathroom, dressing room, and private patio—but no television or telephone to disturb the peace. So how do you request room service or privacy? Raise a flag. Each cottage has a flagpole outside that someone watches from the main area of the resort—raise the red flag and the resort knows that no staff is supposed to come near your area; raise the yellow flag, leave a note stating what you want and when you want it, and *voilà!* all your desires are fulfilled.

A daiquiri on the beach at two o'clock? No problem. Breakfast arranged on the patio for when you return from your early morning skinny-dip? Just ask. And don't worry about the staff catching you in an awkward position—as they near the cottage, they ring a bell out front to warn you.

Although the main activity is the beach and each other, there are some other recreational opportunities, including water sports, tennis courts, recreational trails, and the option to charter a boat to get off the island. You can take your meals in your cottage or in the main pavilion with others, and some evenings feature events such as a cocktail party with the island's owner or a beach barbecue. In the bar, you can mingle with other guests and those yachting in the area who stop in for a drink. Yes, seriously.

Bermuda

LOCATION: six-hundred-fifty miles off the coast of Cape Hatteras, North Carolina

HIGH SEASON: May–October LOW SEASON: November–March
CONTACT: Bermuda Department of Tourism, 310 Madison Avenue, New York, NY 10017; (800) 223-6106, (212) 818-9800; fax: (212) 983-5289
http://www.bermudatourism.com

Pink sand beaches and a decidedly British flair characterize Bermuda, the oldest British colony. Bermuda is actually a chain of seven large islands and some 150 smaller ones off the coast of North Carolina, with the large ones connected by bridges and causeways, creating the illusion of one island. Although Bermuda is frequently grouped with islands in the Caribbean and the Bahamas, it is quite different in many ways.

The first, and possibly most important difference for planning purposes, is that its prime season is the exact opposite of most other area islands. Bermuda is most popular (with correspondingly higher prices) during the summer months when temperatures hover pleasantly in the high seventies. While the winter months remain temperate, the air—mostly in the sixties and low seventies—becomes too cool for the beach, although ideal for golf, tennis, and other outdoor activities.

Because of its British colonial heritage, Bermuda comes off as more formal than most other islands, with an understood dress code that's conservative, although hardly unreasonable by most standards: Bathing suits, for example, are not appropriate even for outdoor activities like bicycling, and in the evenings, many restaurants require men to wear a jacket and tie. And if you've got a pair or two of Bermuda shorts tucked away in the back of your closet, yes, they really do wear them here; in fact, they (or slacks or a skirt) are required on the golf courses.

Bermuda has several good beaches, most free, with the most popular being Horseshoe Bay, complete with toilets, showers, and other public facilities; John Smith's Bay, with stunning views and small caves along one end; and Church Bay, a small, sandy cove on the South Shore, popular for snorkeling and fishing, also with public facilities. All told, there are more than eight hundred acres of protected reserves, parks, and beaches, so you can always do some exploring and find a private area.

In terms of accommodations, Bermuda has several top-notch resorts, but also consider a stay at one of its "cottage colonies": private white-roofed cottages grouped around a main clubhouse with a dining room and other facilities. Most either sit on the beach or have a pool.

Bora Bora

LOCATION: Tahiti, Leeward Society Islands, South Pacific
HIGH SEASON: June–August LOW SEASON: September–December
CONTACT: Tahiti Tourisme, 300 Continental Boulevard, Suite 180, El Segundo, CA 90245; (800) 365-4949, (310) 414-8484; fax: (310) 414-8490
http://www.tahiti-tourisme.com

The very name "Bora Bora" conjures images of an exotic tropical island where you check your cares at the door. And in one of those strange quirks of fate, the island really does live up to its image. Just eighteen miles around, the tiny volcanic island is an unbelievable tropical paradise with lush green foliage and powdery white sand, surrounded by ocean waters that seem to take on every possible nuance of blue. The very air is sensuous, strongly perfumed by the tropical flowers, and heavy and damp (don't even bother to blow-dry your hair). The sunrise is a mass of colors, and even if you're not normally the kind to get up early enough to see dawn, you probably will here. Nightlife is virtually nonexistent.

The island has no real downtown and few restaurants outside of the hotels. The hotels range from average to ultra-deluxe, with the most interesting ones being those with bungalows right over the ocean. Usually the thatched bungalows are connected by a common dock and come complete with mask, fins, and snorkel so you can dive right into the water from your room!

If you do care to venture from your hotel, the entire circumference of the island has interesting beaches and great diving, from Raititi Beach in the south, where the island's first hotel (Hotel Bora Bora) was built, to the White Valley in the north where the coral attracts a range of fish, including parrot fish and soldier fish. Not for the faint of heart, but definitely unusual, are the shark feeding excursions: You actually get out of the boat and into the water while the guide feeds the sharks. As long as they stay on their side of the rope and you stay on yours, everybody's happy.

Positano

LOCATION: Amalfi Coast, Italy; south of Naples
HIGH SEASON: April-October LOW SEASON: November–March
CONTACT: Italian Government Tourist Board, Rockefeller Center, 630 Fifth Avenue, New York, NY 10111; (212) 245-4822; fax: (212) 586-9249

Positano is one of those spots that time has somehow managed to bypass, with whitewashed Moorish-style houses clinging to the terraces of a hillside that overlooks the Mediterranean Sea. One of numerous charming small towns along the Amalfi Coast in central Italy, Positano was described as a "dream place" by the writer John Steinbeck, an image that lives on today. Despite the tourism boom that took place after the Second World War, Positano still retains a peaceful flavor, its winding streets lined with low-roofed white houses and surprisingly elegant boutiques. The town is surrounded by green mounts, while at its feet are two beaches and a colorful and busy fishing port.

Of a handful of area hotels, the sixty-room Hotel San Pietro (phone: 39-89-875455; fax: 39-89-811449), perched high on the rocks above the sea, has become particularly popular with honeymooners and others looking for a romantic getaway. The hotel has its own private beach, where the ocean is colored an even deeper green than the Caribbean with tinges of blue.

From the resort itself, atop the cliff, you can either ride an elevator down to the beach or take the hundreds of steps down. (Note: The roads that lead up to the hotel are so windy and narrow that Dramamine is actually recommended.) The third and most popular option is to stake a claim on a site on the cliff and simply dive into the ocean from the cliffside.

Other than the beach, the main attractions are exploring the town of Positano, where colorful cottons and silks flap in the breeze beside small boutiques, and an excursion along the narrow, twisting Amalfi Drive, with some of the most spectacular views in all of Europe. Be sure to stop in the town of Amalfi, where the tall white houses perch on slopes facing the sea and vaulted passageways lead to quaint, small squares with fountains.

Corfu

LOCATION: Most northern of the Ionian Islands, Greece
HIGH SEASON: May–September LOW SEASON: October–April
CONTACT: Greece National Tourist Office, 645 Fifth Avenue, New York, NY 10022; (212) 421-5777; fax: (212) 826-6940 http://www.compulink.gr/tourism

Unlike most Greek islands, which are craggy and brown, Corfu is green year-round, blessed with countless cypress groves and millions of olive trees. Although the island has a rich history—more Italian than Greek, with a soupçon of Russian, French, and English—that's not what draws visitors. Couples from the world over flock here simply because the island is one of the most beautiful in the world.

Sailing into the port of Corfu, you get a spectacular view of its Venetian-style charming main town, called Corfu Town or Kérkyra, tucked in protectively between two Venetian forts. Wander around town a bit and you can get a flavor of most of the ruling nations of Europe: an arcade that imitates the Rue de Rivoli from the French, a cricket field courtesy of the British, and ancient Greek ruins. Out-of-town sightseeing revolves around Kanoni, from where you can walk out to Vlacherna, the little island monastery whose facade has become virtually synonymous with Corfu, and the Achillion, the former palace of Empress Elisabeth of Austria, its ugliness one of the few blights on the beautiful island.

Experiencing Corfu's different beaches can keep you busy for days. Since the whole island is less than forty miles long, it's easy to explore a different beach area each day if you rent a car. Highlights include Pelakas with its black eroded rocks; Phaliraki, a rocky beach beneath the grounds of Mon Repos, the royal villa where Prince Philip, the Duke of Edinburgh, was born; Paleokastritsa, where an ancient monastery overlooks a row of restaurants and coves on the northwestern coast; and Aghios Gordis, a popular resort area along a bay on the west coast.

St. John

LOCATION: three miles from St. Thomas (twenty minutes by ferry); United States Virgin Islands

HIGH SEASON: December–April LOW SEASON: June–September

CONTACT: U.S. Virgin Islands Division of Tourism, 1270 Avenue of the Americas, New York, NY 10020;

(212) 332-2222; fax: (212) 332-2223
http://www.usvi.net

Only nineteen square miles and the smallest of the three U.S. Virgin Islands (St. John, St. Thomas, and St. Croix), St. John consistently ranks among the top island vacation spots in survey after survey. Unlike its larger counterparts, St. John remains largely undeveloped; two-thirds of the island is a national park, established in 1956 on land donated by Laurence Rockefeller. Nature lovers can choose from more than twenty hiking trails, wending their way among more than eight hundred species of trees, shrubs, and other plants.

Even the most luxurious resort on the island, Caneel Bay, respects the environment, its upscale ambiance skillfully blending into a magnificently landscaped 170 acres, including seven of the best beaches on the island. Although technically all beaches on the island are open to the public, six of Caneel Bay's white-sand beaches are only accessible via water to those without the means to stay at the resort. The seventh, Hawksnest Beach, a narrow and windy gem beautiful enough to have captured the eye of several filmmakers, is accessible by land and does become crowded.

Likewise, the island's other best-known beach, Trunk Bay, is often packed with tourists. With palms and sea grapes in the background and rich snorkeling right off its beach, it's become a favorite for cruise ship stopovers and daytrippers from St. Thomas. Large underwater signs identify the species of coral and other sights along the way.

There's also good snorkeling (without the crowds) off the long sandy beach of Cinnamon Bay, which adjoins a national park campground. The beach at Salt Pond Bay is more secluded (its only facilities are one outhouse and a few picnic tables). The bay there is calm with good snorkeling, but the beach is rockier than the others.

The choice of accommodations on St. John is rather limited—a couple of high-end resorts, two campgrounds, and a handful of budget inns and eco-resorts, as well as condominium and villa rentals. Cruz Bay is the only town on the island, but despite its small size (the streets don't even have names), a number of artisans have chosen to set up shop there, displaying items ranging from handcrafted jewelry to hand-blown glass to tribal masks.

Matangi Island

LOCATION: Private island of Fiji; 190 miles northeast of Nadi, site of Fiji International Airport
HIGH SEASON: April–December LOW SEASON: January–March
CONTACT: Matangi Island Resort of Fiji, 5721 Arapahoe Road, Suite AI, Boulder, CO 80303;(888) MATANGI, (303) 417-0552; fax: (303) 417-0557
http://www.matangiisland.com
Fiji Visitors Bureau, 5777 Century Boulevard, Number 220, Los Angeles, CA 90045; (800) 932-3454, (310) 568-1616; fax: (310) 670-2318
http://www.fijifvb.gov.fj

A 240-acre privately owned island, Matangi Island is a romantic ideal, with only eleven *bures*—typical Fijian-style bungalows—nestled under the palms and gardens redolent with the fragrance of wild orchids, frangipani, hibiscus, and ginger plants. Each bure is within easy walking distance of the dining and activities center and of the soft, white sand beach, but all are far enough from each other to provide privacy even on the beach directly in front of your bure. In keeping with the lush tropical surroundings, the bures are simple affairs, with bedrooms that include mosquito netting and fans rather than air conditioning. The services and amenities are top-notch, though, with well-stocked minibars, free pickup and cleaning of clothing, nightly turn-down service, and more.

The secluded beach is the main attraction here, ideal for spending time with each other and soaking in the glorious aquamarine waters. But if you want activity, it's readily available. Right off the beach is great snorkeling and shore dives, with dive excursions arranged by the resort to the exquisite soft corals for which the north of Fiji is famous. Trips can also be arranged to the magnificent Horseshoe Bay, accessible only by boat; around Matangi and neighbor islands during sunset cruises; and to the bush for treks where you can spot red-breasted parrots or barking pigeons as well as a variety of other native birds, and some cows, goats, pigs, and wild horses that remain from the island's former life as a working plantation.

The resort also schedules tours to the island of Qamea where you can observe the lifestyle of villagers and even participate in a Kava ceremony, where you sample the drink that was formerly reserved for chiefs and is now considered the national drink. (Kava has a calming effect on the body, but unlike alcohol, leaves the mind clear and doesn't produce hangovers!)

If you're coming to Mantangi for a honeymoon or other special occasion, consider booking the Treehouse Bure. Rising thirty feet off the ground in the branches of a large Pacific almond tree, it really is a treehouse, providing a fantasy world of exquisite views and absolute privacy.

Tenerife

LOCATION: One of the Canary Islands, Spain

HIGH SEASON: December–March LOW SEASON: June–August

CONTACT: Tourist Office of Spain, 666 Fifth Avenue, New York, NY 10022; (888) OK-SPAIN, (212) 265-8822;

fax: (212) 265-8864
http://www.okspain.org

Tenerife is ideal for couples who want that oh-so-difficult-to-find blend of amenities and nature, nightlife and tranquility, sophistication and a bit of the unknown. If that's not enough, it even throws in a touch of history and mystery in the form of *los Guanches*, the native race that inhabited the islands before the Spanish arrived. When they were "discovered," they were literally still living as if in the Paleolithic era (better known as the Stone Age): They did not wear clothing, had no language but a series of whistles, made their homes in caves, and, despite living on an island, did not know how to sail. Yet they mummified their dead, a tradition found elsewhere only among the Peruvians and the ancient Egyptians. And, oh yes, in this remote island off the coast of Africa, these people were tall, big boned, and blond.

Speculation runs rampant: A Viking expedition thrown off course? A lost tribe? The last remaining descendants from Atlantis? No one knows, but it's a perfect topic of conversation while lounging on the beach. Most tourists stay at the southern end of the island, where the temperature is warm and dry, rather than the northern part, which is rainier, cooler, and greener.

Among the new hot spots is the Costa Adeje, ten minutes from the airport, where elegant resort complexes front wide yellow-sand beaches that offer windsurfing, sailing, diving, waterskiing, and, of course, plain old swimming and sunning. Nearby are the giant cliffs of Los Gigantes and the Canadas del Teide national park, with its spectacular volcanic landscape of solidified lava forms. During the winter, you can look up at the snow-capped peak of Teide, the highest mountain in Spain, from the sun-drenched beach.

Beaches follow the curve of the island, so it's easy to get out and explore new ones away from the resorts. Among the most popular are the Playa Jardin, at Puerta de la Cruz, a long man-made beach divided into three parts by the rocks (the northern part is free of the rocks that line the southern part, closer to town); El Bullolo, near Puerta de la Cruz, surrounded by cliffs and banana plantations; and Las Teresitas, the most popular on the island among locals. Twenty minutes from Santa Cruz, Las Gaviotas Beach has a nude section and a gay section, along with some rustic facilities.

Palm Beach

LOCATION: Aruba, Southern Caribbean
HIGH SEASON: December–April LOW SEASON: May–November
CONTACT: Aruba Tourism Authority, 1000 Harbor Boulevard, Weehawken, NJ 07087; (800) TO-ARUBA, (201) 330-0800; fax: (201) 330-8757
http://www.interknowledge.com/aruba

Aruba is a good deal at pretty much any time, but two factors make it particularly appealing during its summer off season. First, its location in the southern Caribbean places it firmly outside of the Hurricane Belt. Second, its temperatures are a fairly steady average of eighty-two degrees year-round. So why is the summer even low season when there's no reason not to go then? Guilt by association—since most other Caribbean islands aren't at their peak during the summer, most travelers just lump Aruba into the same category.

In fact, not only is Aruba out of the Hurricane Belt, it barely gets any rain at all—a mere twenty inches a year, most of it during short showers in November and December. The combination of the dryness and the almost constant trade winds conspire to keep Aruba comfortable at almost all times, meaning that you can go on the beach and bask in the sun without breaking into a sweat. A warning, though: Those same winds that keep you cool can wreak havoc on hairdos, hairpieces, and dresses (trust me on this one—do not attempt to wear a short, wide skirt in Aruba).

The most popular beach for tourists is Palm Beach on the west coast, along which most of the major resorts are lined. Most of the east coast is off limits for swimming because of fierce waves, but a little gem at the southeast tip, Boca Grande, doesn't get many beach-goers and is ideal for snorkeling and for being at one with nature and each other.

When the sun sets, there's a flurry of activity all over the island. Many of the large resorts have their own casinos, nightclubs, and shows (indoor and outdoor under the stars), most of them within walking distance of each other along Palm Beach. Another center of activity is downtown Oranjestad, a pretty little area with pastel-colored buildings where the Dutch influence is strong. The island also features a surprising number of truly fine restaurants, among them the romantic Chez Mathilde, located in a nineteenth-century home, and Papiamento, with a beautiful outdoor garden.

Kapalua Beach

LOCATION: Northwest Maui, Hawaii
HIGH SEASON: November–April LOW SEASON: June–August
CONTACT: Hawaii Visitors and Convention Bureau,
180 Montgomery Street, Suite 2360, San Francisco, CA 94104;
(800) 353-5846, (415) 248-3800; fax: (415) 248-3808
http://www.gohawaii.com

On the northwest coast of Maui, the beautiful Kapalua Beach, with sparkling, soft white sand dotted with palm trees, is one of the safest beaches on Maui, ideal for swimming in the bay because it's one of the few places on the island that's totally protected from the large waves of rough waters. *Kapalua* roughly translates from Hawaiian as "arms embracing the sea," an apt description of the dramatic lava peninsulas that embrace the coastline to form the crescent-shape beach.

What makes it safe is also what makes it beautiful: The rocky peninsulas along its side, the little island of Molokai so close you can see it clearly, and bayshore reef formations all combine to head off the winds and provide a protected environment. During whaling season, from November through April, it's also a great place to watch the whales go by Molokai, especially from the sides of the bay. Despite the reef, however, visibility isn't all that great for snorkeling, except at the south end.

There are only a couple of very high-end hotels in the immediate area: the Kapalua Bay Hotel, on a classic white-sand beach, and the Ritz-Carlton Kapalua, right next to one of the largest and most ancient burial sites in all of Hawaii. Immediately north of Kapalua is D. T. Fleming Beach Park, a wide beach where the dunes drop sharply and the big waves are good for surfing though not swimming. (Just to confuse matters, locals call Kapalua "Fleming Beach" as well, so make sure you know which one you're talking about before you head out.) For privacy, go just north again to the steep footpaths that lead down to Oneloa Beach (also called Slaughterhouse), a small patch of white-sand beach rimmed by sea cliffs, where locals boogieboard and you can choose a secluded spot for nude sunbathing if you want.

The area is less than ten miles north from the more famous Kaanapali Beach, a tourist fantasy land where some of the grandest hotels on the islands line three miles of white sand. The beach is cut into two sections by the huge lava Black Rock at the Sheraton, where divers and snorkelers congregate to see the fish and eels.

4

Go Your Own Way

The Best Alternative Beaches

Key West

LOCATION: Island sixty miles south of Florida mainland
HIGH SEASON: mid-December–March LOW SEASON: Labor Day–mid-October
CONTACT: Florida Keys and Key West Visitors Bureau, P.O. Box 1147, Key West, FL 33041; (800) FLA-KEYS, (305) 294-2587; fax: (305) 292-7806
http://www.fla-keys.com

The southernmost city of the continental United States, Key West is at the bottom of the Florida Keys, a chain of islands that extends for about 150 miles from the southern tip of Florida into the Gulf of Mexico. It's a vibrant and eclectic town, freewheeling and sophisticated, urbane yet tropical—and very tolerant of all aspects of the gay lifestyle. As early as the 1940s, Tennessee Williams introduced a gay element to the city, which has welcomed gays and lesbians along with all others since then. The attitude's been likened to that of a more laid-back New York City—you can do what you want and no one looks twice.

The city has certainly had its ups and downs. As late as 1934, the government of Florida suggested the bankrupt city be abandoned; today it sees at least one million visitors a year. Interestingly, although the beach is one of the city's main attractions, it doesn't really have great beaches. The two most popular are Smathers Beach, a long, skinny stretch of sand that's actually trucked in from elsewhere, and Fort Taylor, where the beach is made up of rough coral that makes it difficult to get around, especially when attempting to climb into or out of the water. The seaweed and rocks don't seem to stop anyone, though, especially at sunset, when crowds gather to see the spectacular colors.

Fishing, diving, and canoeing through the mangroves are popular pastimes, but they can't compete with the most common one: people-watching, especially at Mallory Square, where crowds gather to watch the sunset and each other. A walking town, Key West is ideal for leisurely strolling and checking out some of the historic sights, such as the house where Hemingway lived, drank, and wrote, and forts that predate the Civil War.

Accommodations run the gamut from upscale resorts to the mid-range chains that line the highway entrance into town and from reasonable motels to homey guest houses within walking distance of the action. Summer used to be low season here, but the area's become increasingly popular with Florida locals who come in for the weekend; reservations are advised during most times of the year.

Orient Beach

LOCATION: French side of St. Martin/St. Maarten, eastern Caribbean

HIGH SEASON: December–February
LOW SEASON: August–September
CONTACT: St. Martin Tourist Office, 10 East 21st Street, Suite 600, New York, NY 10010; (212) 529-8484; fax: (212) 460-8287 http://www.st-martin.org

On the French side of the French/Dutch St. Martin/St. Maarten, Orient Beach is the best-known and largest of several nude beaches on the island. Although clothing is optional on many parts of the mile-and-a-half-long white sand beach, the southern part tends to attract the majority of nude beach-goers, mostly because it's the site of a naturist beach resort, Club Orient.

You don't have to stay at the resort, though, to enjoy the beach; a number of daytrippers from cruise ships as well as guests at other hotels make their way to this part of the beach, in part because it's a nude beach, in part simply because it's a pretty beach. And it's fine if you want to check out the beach without shedding your own clothes—you certainly won't be the only one clothed. Do be aware, however, that there will be naked children and whole families on the beach (visitors from many European countries have quite different attitudes about nudity than the mainstream in the United States).

Orient Beach tends to get somewhat crowded, especially when the cruise ships are in, but it's a nice-size beach and can accommodate the numbers. It features most of the standard amenities, including rental of lounge chairs and pads, restaurants, and a small shopping area, but not the beach vendors that traverse so many Caribbean beaches. There are, however, women who come around to braid hair, and towards the back, you can indulge in the ultimate luxury—an outdoor massage.

The beach fronts on Orient Bay, which is protected by the only barrier reef in the eastern Caribbean, meaning no dangerous currents but enough movement for windsurfing and sailing. Snorkeling is another highlight, as are the three small uninhabited islands in the middle of the bay, perfect for excursions and picnics.

Club Orient is the only nude resort in the area (yes, even meals are taken in the buff), although there are several other resorts, as well as villa rentals, within easy walking and driving distance of the beach. There are also several other clothing-optional beaches on the island, including Baie Rouge, a quiet but rocky beach; Cupecoy, where the water is a little rougher; and Baie aux Prunes, a crescent beach that attracts mostly locals.

Fire Island

LOCATION: Barrier island off Long Island, New York
HIGH SEASON: May–September LOW SEASON: December–March
CONTACT: Fire Island Tourism Bureau, P.O. Box 248, Sayville, NY 11782; (516) 563-8448

Although the thirty-two-mile-long Fire Island actually comprises seventeen different communities, it's really only two of them that gay people talk about when they refer to the island: Cherry Grove and the Pines, separated by a twenty-minute walk through the woods. The Pines is the place for gay men, while lesbians tend to congregate in Cherry Grove, although in the off season, most everyone goes to Cherry Grove, which is slightly larger than the Pines.

In some ways, Fire Island is like an exclusive private club: It's certainly not easy to get to (you can't bring a car to most parts of the island) and once there, you need a lot of money to be able to stay. Because there are virtually no hotels, most people rent out houses, usually as a group, for astronomical prices (a rental for a week could run as high as two thousand dollars in season). So why bother? Because it's the Northeast place to see and be seen for gays and lesbians.

The up side of the fact that people rent out houses is

the meticulous care that's evident in the area. Fire Island is clean and neat, well-kept. Even the beaches don't dare get messy, with seaweed and rocks kept to a minimum, although they have been sorely eroded recently. The communities are all linked with quaint wooden walks and sandy trails, while the eastern side of the island is mostly uninhabited parkland with all sorts of wildlife, including an abundance of deer.

With all the beautiful people there, one might think that the nightlife would be nonstop and wild. It isn't. There are few restaurants and even fewer clubs; the Island Club, the Pavilion in the Pines (right upstairs), and the Ice Palace in Cherry Grove are the main hangouts for drinking and dancing.

Provincetown

LOCATION: Northern tip of Cape Cod, Massachusetts
HIGH SEASON: June–August LOW SEASON: January–February
CONTACT: Provincetown Business Guild (an organization whose sole purpose is to promote gay and lesbian tourism to the area), P.O. Box 421, Provincetown, MA 02657; (800) 637-8696, (508) 487-2313

Provincetown Chamber of Commerce, P.O. Box 1017, Provincetown, MA 02657; (508) 487-3424; fax: (508) 487-8966

When the Pilgrims signed the Mayflower Compact just off Provincetown's shores in 1620, they set the tone of freedom and tolerance that lives on to this day in the town. While Provincetown is certainly not all gay, it is extremely welcoming to gay men and lesbians, and one of the few towns anywhere that has a tourism organization dedicated specifically to gay and lesbian travel (the Provincetown Business Guild).

At the tip of Cape Cod, Provincetown is the smallest of the Cape's towns, only eight square miles. But it packs a lot into that tiny space. The town is still a working fishing village (fresh seafood for dinner!) as well as an artists' colony, and well known for the bohemian spirit that has attracted such writers as Eugene O'Neill, e. e. Cummings, and Jack Kerouac through the years.

The center of town is the main site for lodging and tourists, while the east end is mostly residential and the west end is quiet with numerous small inns. While all the beaches are gay-friendly, the most popular gay beach is Herring Cove, on the west end and fronting spectacular sand dunes. When you hit the beach, head to the left.

Provincetown is on an earlier schedule than many other gay hotspots, with most people making an appearance on the beach as early as 10:00 A.M. and nightlife starting in the late afternoon. Commercial Street, which runs about two miles along the bay from the east end to the west, is packed with restaurants, galleries, boutiques, clubs, and all other manner of entertainment. If money is an issue—or you don't feel like battling the crowds to get into a restaurant—you can always pick up dinner on the street: fried clams, foot-longs, lobsters, chowders, and more. Save at least one night for sunset at the beach—from Herring Cove, the sun appears to set over the water, the only place on the East Coast where it does. Fires are allowed there at night, but you do need to get a permit first.

Sitges

LOCATION: Approximately fifteen miles south of Barcelona, Spain
HIGH SEASON: July–August LOW SEASON: September–May
CONTACT: Tourist Office of Spain, 666 Fifth Avenue, New York, NY 10022; (888) OK-SPAIN, (212) 265-8822; fax: (212) 265-8864
http://www.okspain.org

Sitges has sometimes been likened to Provincetown in that it's a charming little town that appeals to people of all kinds and is quite accepting of gay men and lesbians. A two-thousand-year-old fishing village just outside of Barcelona, Sitges fits the image of small-town Spain to perfection, complete with medieval cobblestone streets, Mediterranean-style houses, and even cliffs and palm trees to enhance that beach feeling.

As in most gay-friendly destinations, it's hard to say exactly why Sitges is so welcoming, only that it is. It draws people from all of Europe, and although small, the town is actually quite cosmopolitan, with signs in all major languages. If you just pop into town without knowing what you're looking for, it's easy to miss the gay scene; it's so much a part of the everyday lifestyle that it just blends in. But take a closer look and you'll see that in this village of some twelve thousand people, there are as many gay bars as in all of Barcelona.

There are numerous gay-friendly and/or gay-owned hotels, restaurants, and bars, and yes, there's a gay beach too. The gay beach, called Ribera, is near the end of Sitges' Old Town, across the street from the Caliopolis Hotel and the Café Pic-Nic. It's hard to miss—just look for the lavender flag. At the southwest end of town, there's a straight nudist beach and just beyond that, a gay nudist beach called l'Home Mort.

You can do Sitges as a daytrip from Barcelona, but be forewarned—the action starts late (as it does in most of Spain for gays and straights) and there could be a problem getting back to Barcelona. If you want to hit the bars and clubs—at least four gay ones are on Calle San Buenaventura—nothing really happens until about 10:00 P.M. at the earliest. Reservations are a must during the high season, especially at popular hotels like the old-world Hotel Romantic (gay and straight) and the elegant Hotel La Renaixenca (mostly gay).

Haulover Beach

LOCATION: North Miami Beach, Florida

HIGH SEASON: December–March LOW SEASON: May–September

CONTACT: South Florida Free Beaches, P.O. Box 330902, Coconut Grove, FL 33133 (include $3 and self-addressed return envelope for an information package); (954) 782-7400 (long distance calls will be returned collect) http://pages.prodigy.net/dimi

Greater Miami Convention and Visitors Bureau, 701 Brickell Avenue, Suite 2700, Miami, FL 33131; (305) 539-3000, (800) 283-2707; fax: (305) 539-3113 http://www.miamiandbeaches.com

While going topless or wearing thong bikinis is accepted along many Miami beaches, part of Haulover Beach, a mile and a half stretch of white sand three miles south of the Broward County line, is notable as a large and well-respected clothing-optional beach. The clothing-optional part is generally packed with beach-goers who can number in the thousands during the high season, marking a distinct change from the neighboring beaches, which typically don't attract large crowds. The northern part of the beach is primarily gay.

Unlike many nude beaches, which can be small, out-of-the-way, and not necessarily officially sanctioned, Haulover is paroled by well-trained lifeguards and even the police, and features all the important amenities: restrooms, showers, concessions for food and suntan lotion (a necessity!), and parking right across the street for less than five dollars. Also across the street from the beach is Haulover Park, with a full-service marina, restaurant, tennis courts, and family nine-hole golf course.

"Clothing optional," of course, means just that, and there are some in full or partial bathing suits. Even those who opt for no bathing suits typically wear shoes—the sand is *hot* here! Despite the official protection—or perhaps because of it—most people on this beach are comfortable and very aware of the rules and traditions of the beach. There's a prevailing sense of safety and camaraderie. And it's a good thing, because the beach is crowded—you might find yourself within two feet of another person or group. There are, however, the occasional gawkers—those who come to look in a way that might make you feel uncomfortable. If you find yourself faced with one, confrontation is probably not your best bet—either inform an official or move.

Mykonos

LOCATION: Aegean Islands, Greece
HIGH SEASON: May–October LOW SEASON: February–March
CONTACT: Greece National Tourist Organization, 645 Fifth Avenue, New York, NY 10022; (212) 421-5777; fax: (212) 826-6940
http://www.compulink.gr/tourism

Some say Mykonos is out of style for gay travelers, but they're the ones who haven't been there for a while. Mykonos is back and hotter than ever for gay and lesbian beach-lovers. Which is, of course, not to say that the island doesn't attract a healthy number of straight travelers—it is, after all, renowned as one of the most stunning of all the fabulous Greek isles—just that all types work and play well together here.

With the white, white of the houses, old-fashioned windmills, and even the streets rising on hills against the blue, blue of the sky, Mykonos dazzles the eye. Then, when you start trying to find your hotel, restaurant, or anything else in the main town, also called Mykonos, it boggles the mind. The streets are narrow and winding and either don't have names or have names that change every block or so. None will match any official literature you might have picked up beforehand. How do you find a place? Ask, and ask again, and then try one more time.

Whether the nightlife is good is open to interpretation: Some say it's hot, some say it's practically nonexistent. Judge for yourself, starting at the most renowned (although no longer exclusively) gay spot, Pierros. Don't like it? Don't worry—there are three other gay/gay-friendly possibilities in the same building, as well as others throughout town.

As for the gay beaches, they tend to be the ones farthest from town. The most popular are Super Paradise, a crescent of sand bordered by cliffs, where nude bathing is not only allowed but preferred, and Paradise, one beach closer to town, where gays and straights mix. In recent years, Elia Beach, the farthest from town along this stretch, has started to attract those looking for a more secluded and less populated spot. The beaches can be reached by bus or boat from the harbor.

Pattaya

LOCATION: South of Bangkok, Thailand
HIGH SEASON: October–January LOW SEASON: May–August
CONTACT: Tourism Authority of Thailand, 303 East Wacker Drive, Suite 400, Chicago, IL 60601; (800) THAILAND, (312) 819-3990; fax: (312) 565-0359
http://www.tat.or.th

Although the government of Thailand is trying very hard to play down the seamier side of Pattaya, instead promoting it as a resort for couples, families, and even corporate meetings, Pattaya has held firm to its roots. A two-hour drive from Bangkok, what was originally a sleepy fishing village used to attract a handful of Thais who wanted to get away from it all. But when American soldiers discovered Pattaya during the Vietnam War, the town quickly adjusted to the new demands of these men seeking R&R.

When the war ended, the city again transformed itself, this time into an international resort, one of the most popular in Asia with more than twenty-five thousand hotel rooms in nearly three hundred hotels. Pattaya's dark side is still alive and well, however, with estimates of some four thousand "working girls" plying their trade to a willing consumer base that comes from all over the world. (Please do keep one thing in mind: Thailand has one of the highest incidences of AIDS in all of Asia.)

Pattaya fronts the Gulf of Siam, with a palm-fringed white-sand beach that curves into a U. The north side of the beach is mostly hotels, ranging from simple bungalows to world-class resorts, while the south end has one of the highest concentrations in the world of bars, discos, cabarets with female impersonators, strip joints, massage parlors, prostitutes, and transvestites. The action starts when the sun goes down, and out come the portable food stalls and vendors selling everything from Buddhas to leather belts to the accompaniment of blaring music. Another main road runs parallel to the beach road with a number of smaller roads connecting the two; all are lined with restaurants, bars, and shops.

Despite all the adult entertainment, Pattaya actually does attract a healthy mix of other tourists, primarily for the water sports, ranging from snorkeling to windsurfing, and the fifteen world-class golf courses. If the high voltage of Pattaya gets to be too much, the beach Jontien is just to the south and much quieter, and there are a number of nearby offshore islands that are easy to get to for daytrips, including Koh Larn, the largest and popular for snorkeling and scuba diving, and farther out, Koh Lin, Koh Phai, and Koh Sak, with better coral and even fewer people.

Rehoboth Beach

LOCATION: Southern Delaware eastern shore
HIGH SEASON: June–August LOW SEASON: November–March

CONTACT: Rehoboth Beach–Dewey Beach Chamber of Commerce, P.O. Box 216, Rehoboth Beach, DE 19971-0216; (800) 441-1329, (302) 227-2233; fax: 302-227-8351
http://www.dmv.com/business/rehoboth

Although Rehoboth Beach has been a gathering place for gay men and lesbians since the 1960s, the town underwent a kind of crisis during the mid-eighties and early nineties as it tried to reconcile its family image with a growing influx of gay visitors. Rehoboth police now go through sensitivity training each summer, and the town appears to have settled on a win-win approach: Beachgoers along the central part of Rehoboth's beach are primarily families and couples, while at the south end of the boardwalk is Poodle Beach, mostly for gay men. More recently, lesbians have claimed the north end of the beach, formerly Whiskey Beach, now named North Shores and nicknamed Dinah's Shore.

Rehoboth has accommodations in all price ranges and styles and at least fifteen motels and guesthouses that cater specifically to a gay clientele. Most businesses in Rehoboth now consider themselves gay-friendly, and there are at least one hundred area businesses that are either gay-owned or aggressively court gay business. Among them are some thirty restaurants, bars, and clubs, including the Blue Moon, an outdoor bar for gay men with an enviable center position on Baltimore Avenue, an area that's virtually an outdoor gay mall; Plumb Loco, a bar/grill with live entertainment and mostly a lesbian crowd on First Street; and Renegade, a disco at the Renegade Resort that attracts gay men and lesbians with light shows, drag, male burlesque, and karaoke.

Rehoboth's boardwalk stretches for one mile along the beach and is busy at all hours of the night and day with people exploring its shops, restaurants, and arcades; an especially popular section is where the boardwalk intersects Rehoboth Avenue, lined with its own boutiques and eateries. Along Route 1 are some of the country's busiest outlet malls, featuring good prices and no sales tax.

Venice Beach

LOCATION: Southern California; ten minutes from Los Angeles
HIGH SEASON: June–August LOW SEASON: December–March
CONTACT: Los Angeles Convention and Visitors Bureau, 685 South Figueroa Street, Los Angeles, CA 90017; (213) 624-7300; fax: (213) 624-1992

Unlike any other place in the world, Venice Beach is known for its artists, street performers, and uniquely funky atmosphere. It's like walking through a carnival that runs year-round, featuring a friendly cross-cultural mix of arts and crafts, piercing and tattooing salons, and folding tables offering literature on a wide range of grassroots organizations and independent politics. As for live entertainment, the boardwalk is the gathering place for local comics, jugglers, musicians, sidewalk artists, bodybuilders, and roller skaters.

Venice's unconventional reputation began in the early 1920s, when the community became "The Playland of the Pacific." Founder Abbot Kinney envisioned Venice as an environment that would foster a cultural renaissance in America. He commissioned two architects to design the city and residences, complete with amusement piers, Venetian-style structures, and sixteen miles of canals to clinch the resemblance to Venice, Italy. The few original canals that remain today are in a quaint upscale neighborhood with fully restored and remodeled homes.

In the sixties, artists and hippies made rock bands and pot parties the norm in Venice. Before the Doors became famous as the epitome of youth subculture, the band was playing to local kids in Venice and living in a tumbledown house on the canal. So little had changed by the 1990s that Hollywood director Oliver Stone brought his production crew back to Venice to film the history of Jim Morrison and the Doors, using locals as authentic-looking extras.

In the best spirit of the counterculture, you can get a room by the beach or a good meal cheaper than almost anywhere else along the southern California coastline. Accommodations range from luxurious resorts to the Venice Beach Hostel, which offers a "Dorm Special" for fifteen dollars a night. If you are a "talented and creative artist" who paints, sculpts, writes, or performs, you may even qualify for subsidized lodging at the hostel!

Part II

On the Go

5

Hang Ten

The Best Beaches for Surfing

Biarritz

LOCATION: Southwest France
HIGH SEASON: June–August LOW SEASON: December–February
CONTACT: French Government Tourist Office,
444 Madison Avenue, 16th Floor, New York, NY 10022;
(900) 990-0040 ($.50/minute); fax: (212) 838-7855
http://www.francetourism.com

The palace that Napoléon III built for Eugénie still stands as testimony to the honored position Biarritz once held in European society. Now, though, it's a deluxe hotel (appropriately called the Hotel du Palais), in its own way still a symbol of the current role of Biarritz—a mecca for those seeking the sun and the surf. Its glory may be faded (some say nonexistent), but its surf is still as strong as the day in the 1950s that Peter Vietel, scriptwriter and husband of actress Deborah Kerr, first surfed the waves in Biarritz and then proceeded to introduce the town to surfing pioneers and champions.

While some argue that Biarritz is not the best place in Europe for surfing, there's no doubt that it's the most popular, attracting surfers and spectators from all over the world to the annual Biarritz Surfs Masters every September. The city's temperate climate, warmed by the Gulf Stream, allows for swimming from April through October and surfing year-round, with the best conditions in the autumn. It does get crowded during the summers, though, with colorful beach tents packed tightly next to each other.

If you can tear yourself away from the beach, you'll find that Biarritz is in the center of a fascinating area: Basque country, where the local population is neither quite French, nor exactly Spanish, and has somehow managed to survive as a distinct group dating from a time that can't even be figured anymore. The Pyrenees are right there, and if you go four-wheel-driving through them, you'll end up crossing and recrossing the borders between France and Spain. The Bordeaux region, too, is nearby, with tours and tastings available at area wineries. Still yearning for the ocean? Try a warm sea-water treatment at any of five area thalasso-therapy centers, designed to aid a host of ailments.

Guincho

LOCATION: Central west coast of Portugal
HIGH SEASON: June–August LOW SEASON: December–March
CONTACT: Portuguese National Tourist Office, 590 Fifth Avenue, New York, NY 10036; (800) PORTUGAL, (212) 354-4403; fax: (212) 764-6137
http://www.portugal.org

Only about twenty miles west of Lisbon, Guincho is one of a string of beaches that form the Costa do Sol (Sun Coast) or what's sometimes called Portugal's Riviera. Although it's been known among the locals for years, it wasn't until the mid-eighties that this dune-swept windsurfing beach started to gain international renown. Now, all summer long the beach attracts the bright sails of surfers, especially during the annual Guincho Wave Classic, a competitive event that draws surfers from the world over and numerous spectators.

Although Guincho is a favorite with the pros, you do need to know what you're doing to surf here: The Atlantic is wild with currents and an undertow that can be downright treacherous. In fact, the very name *guincho* refers both to the caterwauling cry that the year-round swallows make as they dart in and out of the wildly shifting air currents and the wailing sound of the frenzied sea at night. The beach itself is wide and sandy, with spectacular jutting promontories, and from the beach, you can see Cabo da Roca, the most westerly point on the European continent. Area surfing beaches that are a little tamer include Lagoa do Albufeira, Montargil, and Lagoa do Óbidos.

The hotel selection in Guincho proper is extremely limited, but the town is only four miles from Cascais and six miles from Estoril, two of the most popular beaches on the coast, with numerous hotel possibilities (see chapter 9 for more information about Estoril). Just a couple miles in the other direction is the medieval mountain town of Sintra, with steep winding streets lined with fairytale palaces, ivy-covered mansions, and numerous antique and crafts shops. Here, the hotels range from inexpensive village inns to converted palaces that offer a rare glimpse into the finest of past centuries.

Bondi Beach

LOCATION: Sydney, Australia; twenty minutes from city center
HIGH SEASON: October–April LOW SEASON: May–September
CONTACT: Australian Tourist Commission, 2049 Century Park East, Suite 1920, Los Angeles, CA 90067; (800) 333-0262 (for

brochures only), (847) 296-4900; fax: (847) 635-3718
http://www.aussie.net.au

One of the best-known beaches in Australia, Bondi isn't just a surfer's paradise; it's a "scene" in itself—a must on the list of all those seeking the quintessential Australia beach experience. Ironically, it's barely been a hundred years since swimming during daylight hours was considered unacceptable here, and it's a good guess that those who were disturbed by those bits of naked flesh back then would be utterly appalled by today's topless sunbathers. But time does march on.

Bodysurfing at Bondi was introduced around the turn of the century. By 1906 there were enough people getting into trouble on the Pacific waves that the Bondi Surf Bathers' Lifesaving Club was formed, establishing itself as the oldest surf lifesaving club in the world. Surf lifesavers still patrol the waters, easily identifiable by their red and yellow caps—and their bronzed and muscled bodies. The beach—nearly a mile long—is partitioned with flags so that the swimmers and surfers don't collide; the busiest part of the beach is the central section, with families tending toward the north side near a sheltered saltwater pool.

Just for the record: This is a city beach and although it looks clean, that isn't always the case. Pollution levels are sometimes high enough to prevent swimming safely, so do check out the current status before you dive in.

Lining the beach are hotels, apartment houses, and assorted food and junk shops, lending just a slightly tacky feel to the beach that somehow enhances that one-big-party mood. Bondi's only about ten minutes from the city center, easily accessible by bus, and the Bondi Pavilion Community Center has changing rooms if you prefer not to make the trek decked out for the beach.

The city of Sydney itself is cosmopolitan, sophisticated, and quite international—in short, nothing like the American ideal of the land down under, but providing anything you could want in terms of entertainment, dining, and hotel options.

North Shore, Oahu

LOCATION: Northern beaches of Oahu, Hawaii
HIGH SEASON: November–April LOW SEASON: June–August
CONTACT: Hawaii Visitors and Convention Bureau,
180 Montgomery Street, Suite 2360, San Francisco, CA 94104;
(800) 353-5846, (415) 248-3800; fax: (415) 248-3808
http://www.gohawaii.com

Surfing the mega-waves of the north shore of Oahu is every surfer's dream. Hawaii, of course, is where it all began, with thousand-year-old petroglyphs showing stick figures riding boards. The "father of modern surfing," Olympic swimmer Duke Paoa Kahanamoku, introduced the sport to the world in the early part of this century, but it wasn't until the 1940s that surfboarders dared try the huge winter surf on the north shore.

With the biggest rideable waves in the world, it's no wonder that Waimea Bay Beach attracts huge crowds in the winter—to watch, that is, not to actually surf. Only the most expert surfers should ever attempt to ride these thundering waves. Ironically, during the summer, this same bay can be as calm and smooth as a lake. The other huge challenges on the north shore are Sunset Beach, where the photographers line up in the winter to shoot the experts riding the monster waves, and the Banzai Pipeline, where the waves rise steeply before transforming into tubes that thunder into the reef. Again, these two are only for the pros.

The only north shore beach that's safe for beginner surfers is Haleiwa Beach, and even then only on a gentle day. Other island beaches that are safe for beginning surfers include Waikiki Beach, Ala Moana Beach on the south shore, and Kalana Beach on the windward side.

The north shore is completely unlike the frenzy of Honolulu (a forty-five-minute drive), where most of the island's hotels are based. Here, there are only a few small towns amid the fields of sugarcane, oceanside meadows, and deep lush valleys. There's also only one hotel, a few vacation rentals, and a campground. However, there are numerous boutiques, food stores, and restaurants in the "Gunsmoke"-style wood buildings of Haleiwa, the biggest town in the area.

Besides the beautiful scenery, the only actual sightseeing on the north shore is in Waimea Falls Park, once a center of the ancient Hawaiian religion, where paths wander amid the remnants of temples, homes, and whole villages. Swimming is possible in the natural pool below the falls.

Huntington Beach

LOCATION: Southern California; forty-five minutes south of Los Angeles
HIGH SEASON: June–October LOW SEASON: November–May
CONTACT: Huntington Beach Conference and Visitors Bureau, 101 Main Street, Suite 2A, Huntington Beach, CA 92648; (714) 969-3492; fax: (714) 969-5592
http://www.hbsurfcity.com

Known as "Surf City" and "the blondest place in California," Huntington Beach is the place to see young tanned bodies soaking up the summer sunshine and riding the waves. Since Huntington Beach is a large Orange County suburb, twenty-eight square miles, you'll also see a fair number of stout mamas and grandmamas with kids in tow, lying out alongside the youth culture. But there's plenty of room for everyone on this incredibly long, wide beach that runs for miles along the Pacific Coast Highway.

The community of Huntington Beach is separated from the seemingly endless beach by the Bolsa Chica wetlands, the largest remaining coastal wetlands in southern California. This wide lowland holds graceful egrets and sandpipers, pelicans and plovers, and dozens of other fascinating creatures. Orange County has long drawn ecology-minded people to its vast wetlands, but most of the beachgoers ride right past, noticing only the steel-beam complex of a large power station dominating the marshy landscape.

It's easy to find the heart of Surf City—just go to the Huntington Beach Pier where Main Street begins. Starting at the Pacific Coast Highway, you can walk along the granite stones marking the Huntington Beach Surfing Walk of Fame. You can't miss the International Surfing Museum, home to a collection of some of the most significant artifacts in the history of surfing. Videos of surf music play in the background, or you can listen to live surf bands like the Surfaris, the Reventlos, and the Bone Sharks while viewing the exhibits of memorabilia—surfboards, surf films, surf music, legends of the sport, and even skateboards.

There's plenty to see and do at night in Surf City, but the real action is on Huntington Beach. And with 1,123 hotel rooms in the community, there's no reason not to get your sleep and spend all of your waking time playing in the sun.

Cowell's Beach

LOCATION: Santa Cruz, northern California
HIGH SEASON: June–August LOW SEASON: December–March
CONTACT: Santa Cruz Conference and Visitors Council, 701 Front Street, Santa Cruz, CA 95060; (800) 833-3494,

(408) 423-1111; fax: (408) 425-1260
http://www.scccvc.org

The southern part of California has Huntington Beach, but the northern part has its own "Surf City." Yes, they do both claim the name, and Cowell's Beach in Santa Cruz even has a little more history to back the claim: It was here that surfing was originally introduced to the mainland United States by Duke Paoa Kahanamoku, the Olympic gold medalist from Hawaii, in the 1920s and 1930s. Although it did catch on immediately with some locals, the problem back then was the water temperature, which hovers for most of the year just a few degrees above the freezing point. With the advent of the wet suit, though, that's no longer a problem, and surfers the world over come to ride the large waves.

There's still one other problem, however, that no one's yet been able to fix, and it's a biggie. The waters off the coast of Santa Cruz are among the most notorious Great White Shark feeding grounds in the world. Check out the Santa Cruz Surfing Museum, housed in the Mark Abbott Memorial Lighthouse, where you can watch videos about area surfing and shark attacks, and also see a surfboard with an eighteen-inch shark bite that drives home the point. Still willing to tackle the waters? Then head right outside the museum to the swells of Steamer Lane, one of the most popular and crowded surfing spots in town.

Between the surfing museum and West Cliff Drive is Cowell's Beach, not just popular with surfers but also with sun-worshippers and volleyball players. It's right next to the Beach Boardwalk, a mile-long entertainment stretch where you can ride the 1911 carousel and the 1924 Giant Dipper rollercoaster, eat to your heart's content, and catch free concerts during the summer.

Pleasure Point Beach is another popular area beach

for surfers, while the Twin Lakes State Beach, at the opening of Schwann Lagoon, has some of the warmest waters in the area. At Natural Bridges State Beach where the surf is so strong it's pounded its way right into cliffs, you can see nature in all its glory; if you prefer humans in all *their* glory, try the Red, White, and Blue clothing-optional beach.

If the surf and sand alone aren't enough to set your senses reeling, head inland to Mystery Spot. Balls really do roll uphill here, gravity is upended, trees lean to the side. No, it's not an amusement park—it's just a very strange and inexplicable natural phenomenon that occurs in a redwood grove just north of the city.

Uluwatu

LOCATION: Southwest coast of Bali, Indonesia
HIGH SEASON: June–August LOW SEASON: December–March
CONTACT: Indonesia Tourist Promotion Office,
3457 Wilshire Boulevard, Los Angeles, CA 90010;
(213) 387-8309; fax: (213) 380-4876

With the largest and most reliable swells in Bali, Uluwatu attracts hundreds of jostling surfers from the world over during the summer dry season (June through August). It used to be that you could only get to the beach, technically called Suluban Beach, by walking an arduous two-mile trek from the parking lot next to the Uluwatu temple, but the track was widened a couple of years ago, making it possible for tourists to drive right from the temple to the clifftop overlooking the Indian Ocean surf. In other words, more crowds.

They don't come to swim, however, because there's a huge shallow reef right offshore covered in seaweed. Surfers have to cross the sharp coral to get to the reef breaks, and boots are essential. Still, the small sandy cove retains an atmosphere of easygoing relaxation, and surfers can spend the night (or several) in any of the half-dozen *losmen* (basically small guest houses) back by the cliff wall.

For those who prefer to overnight in a resort atmosphere, the brash and funky Kuta is only a few miles north. One of the biggest tourist towns on Bali, it's also the most untraditional in terms of Balinese culture, a seaside cacophony of *losmen*, hotels, souvenir shops, clubs, bars, and surfers and other international tourists, especially Australians and Japanese. The turquoise waters off the palm-backed wide curve of beach here are also good for surfing, with consistent, almost uniform waves, although not quite as impressive as those at Uluwatu. The waters are also fine for swimming, but with caution because of a strong undertow and breakers. A number of international standard hotels line the beach, while cheaper accommodations tend to be set a few blocks back.

Farther north, Legian used to be a separate town but with all the growth has merged into the general Kuta resort. Still, the town and the beaches are a little less frantic here, and because Legian is in the curve of the beach, it collects the compressed energy of all the swells, providing the most power-packed beachbreaks on the island.

If you happen to be in Bali from December through March, head to the southeast part of the island—Nusa Dur and Sanur—for surfing. It's not as spectacular as the southwest in season, but still better than most. These areas also offer other water sports, such as parasailing, banana boats, and diving and snorkeling.

Bathsheba Beach

LOCATION: East coast of Barbados, part of the Lesser Antilles; eastern Caribbean

HIGH SEASON: December 16–April 15 OFF SEASON: April 16–December 15

CONTACT: Barbados Tourism Authority, 800 Second Avenue, New York, NY 10017; (800) 221-9831, (212) 986-6516; fax: (212) 573-9850
http://barbados.org

On the east side of Barbados, big Atlantic rollers break, striking huge rock formations and forming cascades of foam that hurl onto the wide-open beach. This is Bathsheba Beach, where Bajans (natives of Barbados) and others from around the world gather to ride the rolling waves propelled by the strong eastern wind.

Miles of virtually untouched beach run from Bathsheba north to Cattlewash, providing both a surfing haven and an escape from the more crowded beaches on the west and south shores, where the resorts congregate. But the water here is not for swimming. It's not even for surfing unless you're with people who really know what they're doing: The wild waters run over sharp coral reefs that can be dangerous. The highlight of the area is the Soup Bowl, site of numerous local and international surfing championships, which gets its name from the foamy surf that surrounds it.

Although this part of the island is much quieter than the capital, Bridgetown, in the southwest and the resorts, hotels, and villas that parade north and east from the capital, there are a handful of small inns, mostly catering to surfers and those who want to get away from it all.

In addition to the east coast surfing, Silver Sands at the very southern tip has become well known for windsurfing between November and June, when the wind speed rises to create challenging wave heights between six and fifteen feet.

Although Barbados doesn't have the volcanoes, rain forests, or other exciting geographical features of some other islands, it does have a better infrastructure than many Caribbean islands and more of a sense that real people live here rather than the impression of a fantasy island custom-built for tourism. Bridgetown offers cultural sightseeing, but the best attractions just might be the steep inland cliffs and ridges, sea caves, and arches that run parallel to the coast, creating breathtaking vistas. Harrison's Cave is a must-see (unless you're claustrophobic!): From your seat on an electric tram, you can view magnificent chambers, incredible stalactites and stalagmites, bubbling streams, tumbling cascades, plunging waterfalls, and emerald pools, all created over the course of hundreds of thousands of years from crystallized limestone and rainwater.

Jeffrey's Bay

LOCATION: Eastern Cape; southwest coast of South Africa
HIGH SEASON: November–February LOW SEASON: March–October
CONTACT: South African Tourism Board, 500 Fifth Avenue, Suite 2040, New York, NY 10110; (800) 822-5368, (212) 730-2929; fax: (212) 764-1980
http://www.travelfile.home/get/satour.html

About forty-five minutes south of Port Elizabeth, Jeffrey's Bay, part of St. Francis Bay, attracts local and international surfers with its huge rollers from the Indian Ocean. With seven surf spots in close proximity and a surf window of more than ninety degrees, it also attracts several competitions each year, so even though the area tends to be tranquil and somewhat remote, there are times when the place is packed. But what else could you expect from an area where the surfing spots have names like Super Tubes?

The endless white sand of the beach is also known for accumulating huge numbers of seashells, which wash up daily and are prized by collectors from all over. Accommodations are mostly smaller guest houses and villas for rent; both run the gamut from simple to luxury. A number of campsites are also available in the area.

Although Jeffrey's Bay is a good base for surfing beaches, both in town and north up to Port Elizabeth, you could also hit the town on a tour of the Eastern Cape. Following the beautiful coastal roads of the Garden Route from Cape, you come across several surfing spots, including Elands Bay, Victoria Bay, Mossel Bay, Santos Reef, and those located in Cape Point Nature Reserve.

Not surprisingly, out-of-the-water area attractions center on the area's spectacular natural attractions, and include the Addo Elephant National Park, where Cape buffalo and black rhino share space with 170 elephants; riding horses along the white stretch of beach next to St. Francis Bay; and several other nature reserves that provide protection for crocodiles, snakes, birds, and wildflowers.

Puerto Escondido

LOCATION: Southwest coast of Mexico
HIGH SEASON: December–January, July–August
LOW SEASON: September–November
CONTACT: Mexican Government Tourism Office, 405 Park Avenue, Suite 1401, New York, NY 10022; (800) 44-MEXICO, (212) 421-6655, (212) 838-2949; fax (212) 753-2874 http://mexico-travel.com

In a little beach town that's not known for much else crash the waves of one of Mexico's best surfing spots. So far, Puerto Escondido, south of Acapulco and north of Huatulco, has escaped Mexico's somewhat frantic resort development, apparently in lieu of Huatulco, which *is* being targeted. Good news for surfers, though, who pretty much get the wide cream beaches and the rolling Pacific surf to themselves.

The palm-lined Playa Principal and Playa Marinero,

both right at the town center on a bay, are best for swimming, but surfers head beyond the sharp outcrop of rocks, five minutes east to the two miles of Playa Zicatela. Here's where you'll find what's commonly called the "Mexican Pipeline" in honor of the curling waves that are huge and reliable. Th undertow here is very strong, preventing swimmers but encouraging spectators, especially during August and November, when international surfing championships take place. Unfortunately, the beach has also become a magnet for petty criminals—whether surfer or spectator, don't bring any valuables with you.

The Hotel Santa Fe, right at the beach, has a thatched-roof restaurant where you can watch the spectacular surfers and sunsets while sipping tropical drinks. It's also the only real hotel on the surfing beach; the other accomodations right there range from cabanas with hammocks and shared baths to rooms with a bed, fan, mosquito netting, and private bathroom. Of course, you could always walk back to the main part of town, where hotel options certainly aren't overwhelming but do provide more choice.

Nightlife options are also limited to a handful of bars and clubs, but that's okay because eventually everyone ends up at the same places—mostly Coco for live rock, El Tubo, a beachside disco, and El Son y la Rumba for live Latin music and dancing. Meals tend to the simple side—burgers, spaghetti, and seafood so fresh you'd swear they caught it just for you (and sometimes they do).

6

Dive In

The Best Beaches for Scuba Diving and Snorkeling

Palm Cove

LOCATION: Queensland, Australia; north of Cairns
HIGH SEASON: August–September, December–February
LOW SEASON: October–November, March–July
CONTACT: Australian Tourist Commission, 2049 Century Park East, Suite 1920, Los Angeles, CA 90067; (800) 333-0262 (for brochures only), (847) 296-4900; fax: (847) 635-3718 http://www.aussie.net.au

To explore the Great Barrier Reef, often called the Eighth Wonder of the World, is every diver's dream—1,240 miles of an overwhelming abundance of coral and thousands of species of fish that make it one of the most diverse ecosystems on the planet. If diving is your goal, it almost doesn't matter where you choose to stay on land because most of your time will be spent on daytrips to as many different diving locations as possible.

Still, if getting in some beach time is also important,

Palm Cove offers one of the best beaches in the sixteen-mile sweep north of Cairns, with golden sand, azure waters, and, of course, the eponymous palm trees. Accommodation options are abundant, and the esplanade opposite the beach is lined with small boutiques, alfresco dining options, and more refined full-service restaurants. Many of the reef cruises stop directly at the Palm Cove jetty.

From the mainland, you'll have a choice of several diving options. For experienced divers, the outer reef, which starts about twenty miles from the mainland and borders the open sea, offers the most dramatic possibilities with canyons, cliffs, and the biggest fish. Between the outer reef and the mainland is the inner reef: Flatter, warmer, and more shallow, it's ideal for beginners. There are also numerous islands in the area: the luxurious Hayman Island (one of the Whitsunday Islands); the tiny Green Island, the most accessible of the reef's cays; and Fitzroy Island, only eleven miles from Cairns, to name just a few. In addition to daytrips for diving, many outfits offer longer cruises and diving trips to a combination of inhabited and deserted islands.

Although the coral of the inner reef does show the effects of largely unbridled tourism (the reef has been a World Heritage site since the 1970s), the outer reef remains largely unchanged. The wildlife varies from site to site, ranging from giant potato cod to squid to sharks.

Cozumel

LOCATION: Island off southeastern Mexico, thirty-five miles from Cancún

HIGH SEASON: December–April LOW SEASON: September–November

CONTACT: Mexican Government Tourism Office, 405 Park Avenue,

Carmel-by-the-Sea, California. *Carmel Business Association*

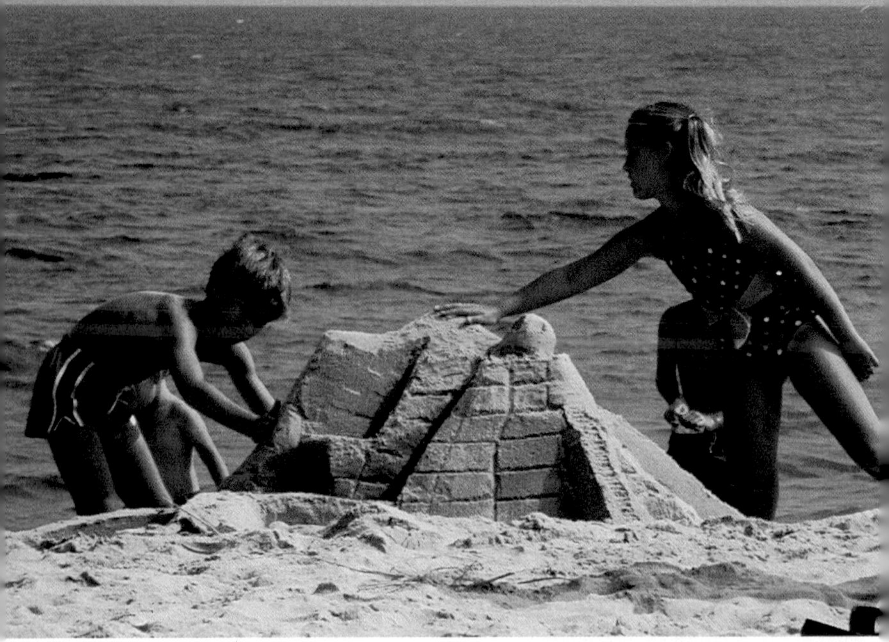

Nantucket. *Nantucket Island Chamber of Commerce*

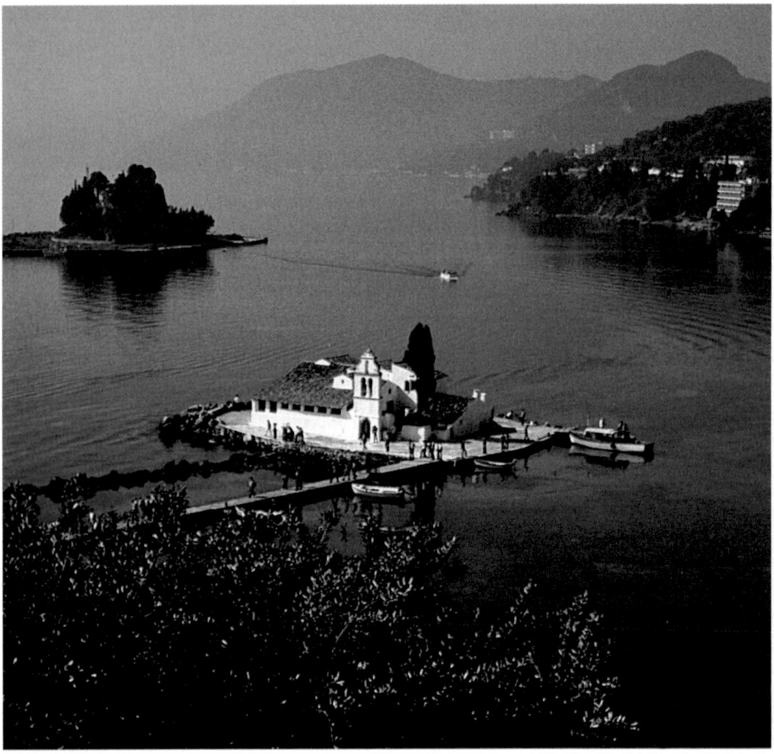

Corfu, Greece. *Greek National Tourist Office*

Nice, France. *French Government Tourist Office*

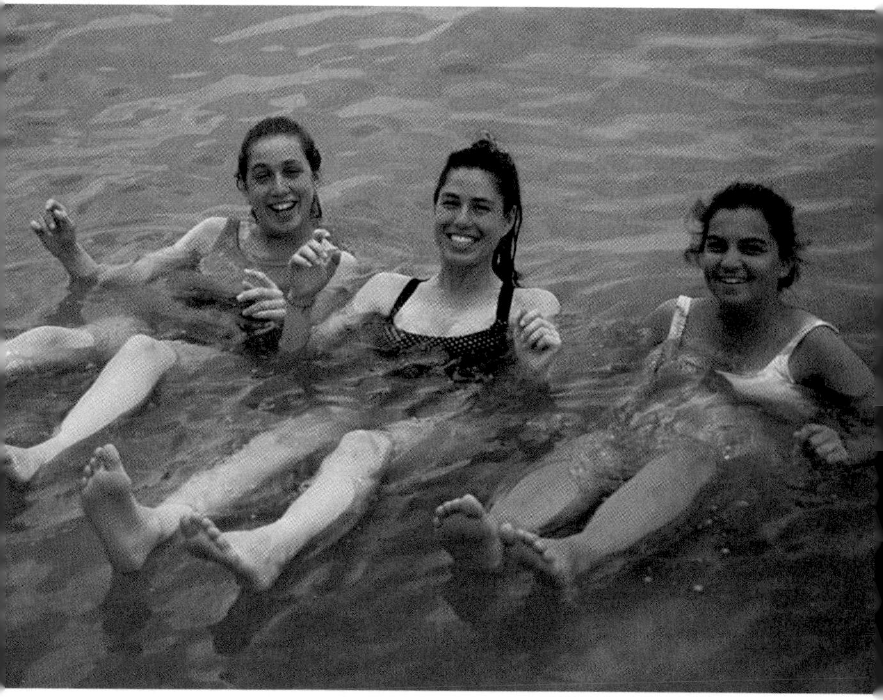

The Dead Sea, Israel. *Israel Ministry of Tourism*

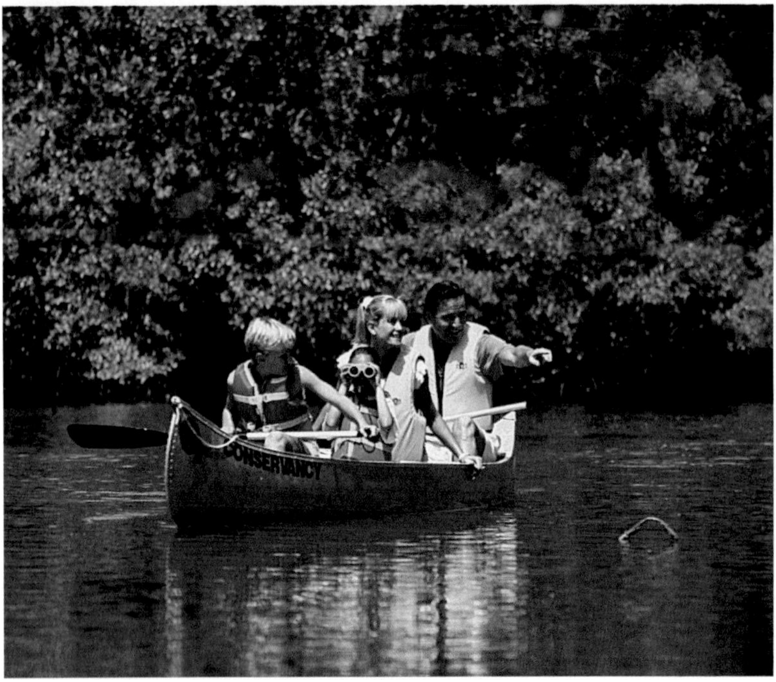

Marco Island, Florida. *Marco Island and The Everglades Convention and Visitors Bureau*

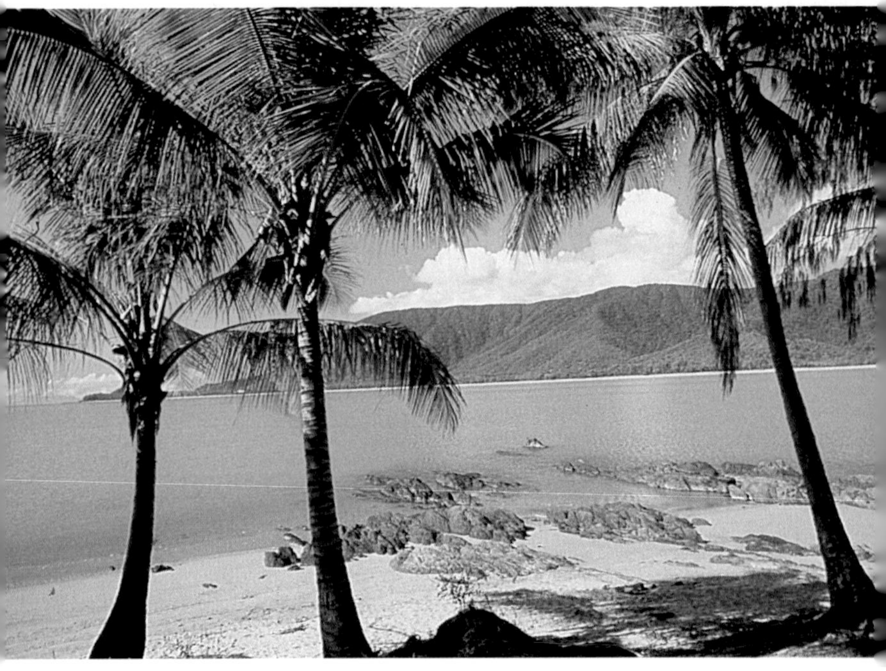
Palm Cove, Australia. *Queensland Tourist and Travel Corporation*

Orient Beach, St. Martin. *St. Martin Tourist Office*

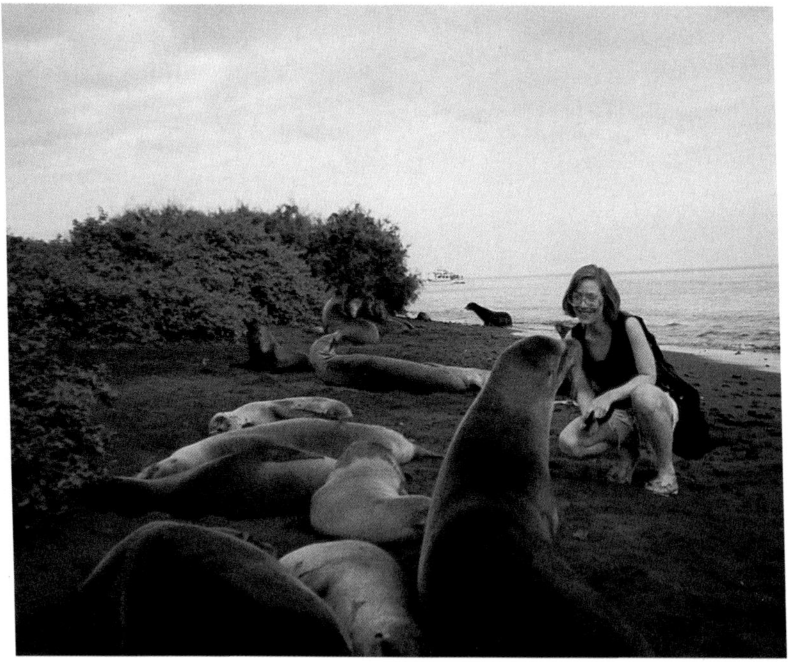

Galapagos Islands. *Photo by Author*

Petit St. Vincent. *Petit St. Vincent Resort*

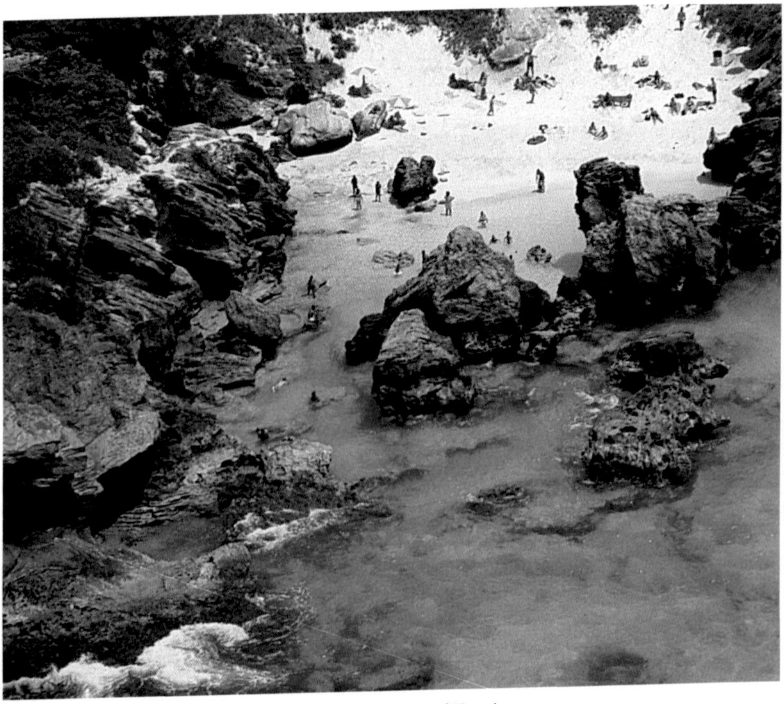

Horseshoe Bay, Bermuda. *Bermuda Department of Tourism*

Provincetown, Massachusetts. *Helen Addison, Provincetown Municipal Advertising Committee*

Gozo, Malta. *Photo by Author*

Tulum (Playa del Carmen), Mexico. *Photo by Author*

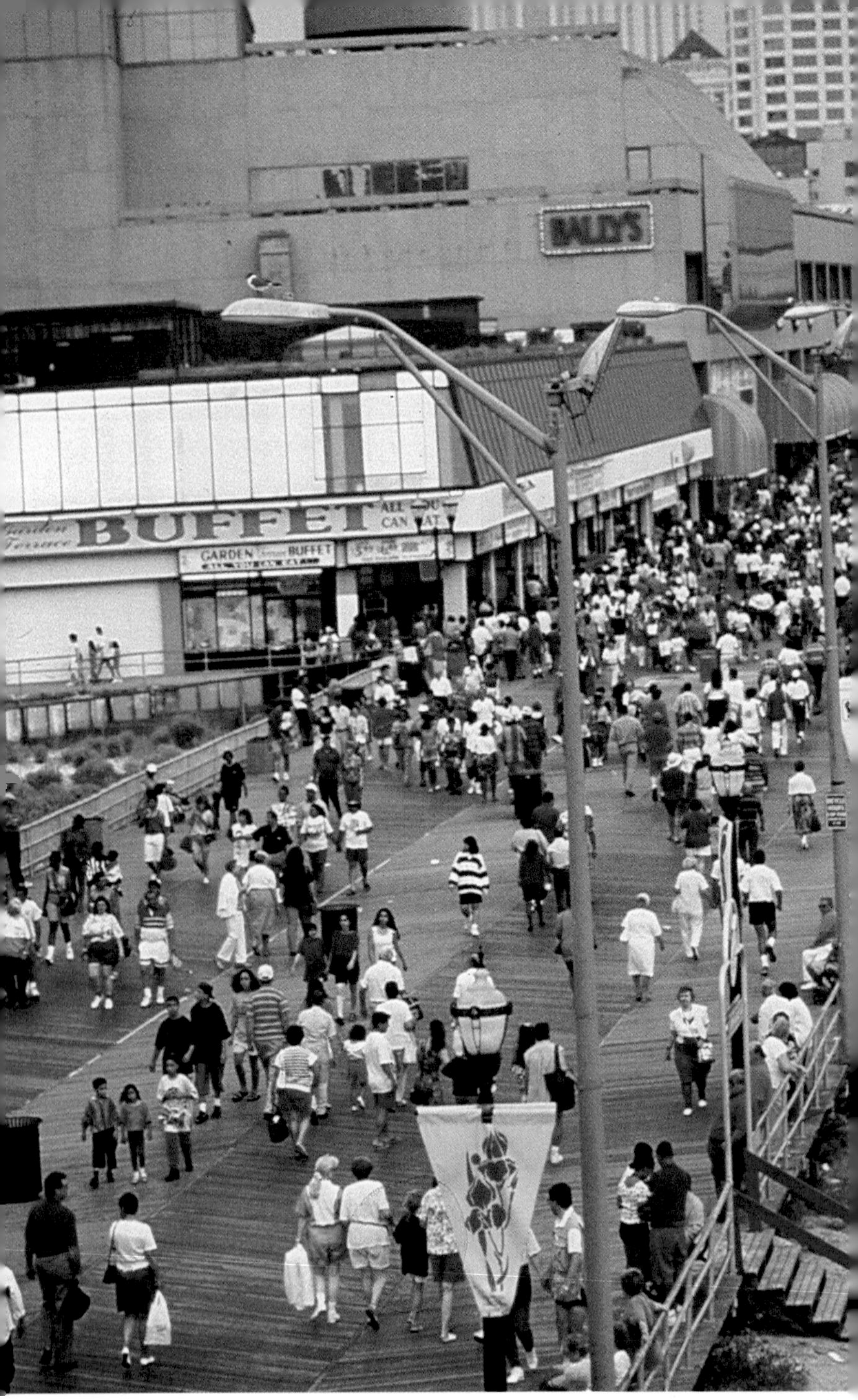

Atlantic City, New Jersey. *Atlantic City Convention and Visitors Bureau*

Suite 1401, New York, NY 10022; (800) 44-MEXICO, (212) 421-6655, (212) 838-2949; fax: (212) 753-2874
http://mexico-travel.com

Considered one of the top five diving sites in the world, Cozumel is a haven for scuba divers, snorkelers, and those who just want a slower pace than the larger and more frenetic Cancún, thirty-five miles away. The island's diving fame started with an endorsement from the renowned Jacques Cousteau in 1961; since then it's become so legendary that a full 35 percent of all visitors are divers.

What draws underwater thrill-seekers is the Gama Reef, the second largest coral reef in the world after the Great Barrier Reef and home to a host of brightly colored tropical fish. Water visibility in the clear Caribbean waters can reach up to two hundred feet, allowing even the timid the chance to view the multihued sealife in all its glory. The hotels are spread out on the west side of the island, the same side as the reef, and those who stay at hotels toward the southern end of the island often can snorkel in the calm blue-green waters off the soft white beaches directly in front of their hotels. The eighteen hotels range from moderate to full-scale luxury, although even the most upper-end tend to be more laid-back than those in comparable resorts.

From May to September, visitors get a spectacular natural show outside the waters when the giant sea turtles lay their eggs on the beaches and exotic migratory birds make pit stops. The island's one town, San Miguel, offers restaurants, shopping, a fourteen-block seaside promenade, and a few of the more moderate hotels, but even in town, the feel is relaxed and casual. If you want to get away from it all even more, the east side of the island is completely undeveloped, and most of the island interior is jungle, perfect for leisurely, albeit careful, exploring. Along the way, stop off at least one of the thirty-five archeological sites, a legacy of the commercial port and ceremonial center of the Mayans who settled on Cozumel in the third century.

Grand Cayman

LOCATION: Cayman Islands, Western Caribbean
HIGH SEASON: November–April LOW SEASON: May–October
CONTACT: Cayman Islands Department of Tourism,
6100 Blue Lagoon, Miami, FL 33126; (800) 327-8777,
(305) 266-2300; fax: (305) 267-2931
http://www.caymans.com

Very clean, very safe, very British, and very expensive, Grand Cayman has more than 160 charted dive sites, but little else in the way of entertainment. Like the two other Cayman Islands—Cayman Brac and Little Cayman—Grand Cayman lies on top of a submerged mountain, and the dive spots offer some of the best visibility in Caribbean—up to two hundred feet in some places. Throughout the three islands, there are more than forty dive operators, offering equipment rentals, instruction, and underwater photography, and diving is well regulated and carefully governed. Many of the hotels also offer diving as part of a package.

Grand Cayman is the most developed of the three islands, though hardly overdone. Although there are several good—and expensive—restaurants on Grand Cayman, there's not much other nightlife besides what the larger resorts serve up in the way of music and dance. Most of the island's hotels line Seven-Mile Beach, where the glasslike turquoise water meets a fine white sand beach. Snorkeling right off the beach in front of the hotels, you can see almost as much sealife as when diving, including turtles, stingrays, and lobsters.

Diving, however, provides some of the most dramatic

views anywhere in the world. At North Wall, for example, you can explore the magnificent reefs, drop-offs of thousands of feet, underwater tunnels and caverns, and a number of shipwrecks. At Stingray City, snorkelers and divers swim freely with thirty friendly stingrays in twelve feet of water.

If you really want to get away from it all, Bloody Bay Wall, off of Little Cayman, has been frequently noted as one of the best dive sites in the world, with a six-thousand-foot underwater drop-off and chutes, chimneys, and caves, as well as coral, sponges, and a variety of sealife, including sharks. There are regular flights from Grand Cayman to the other two islands, and both Little Cayman and Cayman Brac have a handful of resorts of their own.

Sharm el-Sheikh

LOCATION: Southern tip of Sinai Peninsula, Egypt
HIGH SEASON: July–August LOW SEASON: December–March
CONTACT: Egypt Tourist Authority, 630 Fifth Avenue, Suite 1706, New York, NY 10111; (212) 332-2570; fax: 956-6439
http://interoz.com/egypt

At the southern tip of Egypt's Sinai Peninsula, Egypt's most stylish resort is just becoming known among Americans, although it's already a favorite with Southern Europeans. A modern tourist town, Sharm el-Sheikh provides a striking contrast to its surrounding desert areas, which are peopled mostly with Bedouins who live much the same way they have for centuries. A long promenade along the sandy beach links a chain of modern hotels with names that Americans find comforting: Marriott, Inter-Continental, Hilton, and more. Most of the resorts are toward the north of the ten-mile beach area, while the south is less developed.

It's the magnificent coral reefs right offshore in the warm shallows, blazing with all colors imaginable and a stunning variety of technicolor fish, that attract divers and snorkelers. For the moment, that is: Unless the continued development of the area is tempered with some major ecological initiatives, there's a good chance this is one of the diving areas that will soon become only a memory. It's unfortunate, but if you really want to dive here, you'd best go quickly. Despite pollution and desalination, though, locals are acutely aware of the dangers to the marine life of removing five coral from the sea—don't try it.

You can dive directly from most of the hotels on the northern end. Na'ama Beach is the center of the tourist activities, while there are many other diving sites along the ten-mile beach between Sharm el-Sheikh and Ras Nusrani. The country's first national park, Ras Mohammed, is at the southern tip of the peninsula, about a twenty-minute drive from the main resort area. Once an important stopping point for pilgrims on their way to Mecca, the area is now an aquatic paradise for snorkelers and divers. Other sightseeing highlights are Mount Sinai and the famed St. Catherine's Monastery, first settled by hermits in the fourth century A.D. and added to in almost every century since.

Gozo

LOCATION: An island of Malta, Mediterranean Sea

HIGH SEASON: July–September LOW SEASON: October–February

CONTACT: Malta Tourist Office, 350 Fifth Avenue, Suite 4412, New York, NY 10018; (212) 695-9520; fax: (212) 695-8229 http://www.tourism.org.mt

On the west side of Gozo, the northernmost of the three islands of Malta (the name of both the country and the largest island), a long and winding road snakes down to Dwerja, at the bottom of a deep valley where the wind, sea, and flukes of nature have created a rectangular hole nearly three hundred feet wide and sixty feet high through apparently solid limestone. The best way to get your first view of the Azure Window—and the clear blue sea beyond—is from the rocky white cliffs surrounding the window, but for divers, the sights don't stop there.

Right in front of the window is a circular sinkhole, and nearby is a collapsed cave as well as other area caves and grottoes. Although the sea here doesn't sport the masses of exotic tropical fish of some other dive spots, the clear waters provide excellent visibility of white coral and sea creatures ranging from amberjack to lobster and octopus. The waters can be rough, though and accidents do occur—don't try diving in this area on your own.

One of the spots from where diving excursions start is right next to the Azure Window, where the same wild elements have cut a tunnel through the rocky cliffside. On the other side is a tranquil "inland sea," a natural formation that looks almost like a human-constructed pool with a somewhat rectangular formation and pebbly borders (sorry, no sandy beaches here). Sheltered by the tunnel, the pale green waters are warmer than the open sea outside with no waves to disturb the peace. On calm days, fishing boats shuttle divers out through the tunnel to the Azure Window.

Nothing is more than an hour's drive away on the rural little island, so it's easy to stop in for a day at other beach spots, especially the sandy beach at Ramla (overlooked by Calypso's Cave, thought to be where Odysseus was kept as a prisoner of love for seven years in Homer's *Odyssey*) and San Blas, a secluded sandy beach reached down a steep narrow track that keeps most other tourists away.

Bonaire

LOCATION: Netherlands Antilles, Caribbean; fifty miles north of Venezuela

HIGH SEASON: December 15–April 15 LOW SEASON: mid-April–mid-December

CONTACT: Tourism Corporation Bonaire, 10 Rockefeller Plaza, Suite 900, New York, NY 10020; (800) 266-2473, (212) 956-5913; fax: (212) 956-5913
http://www.bonaire.org

One of the few dive spots that's long understood the value of what it has, the island of Bonaire has been protecting its fragile underwater ecosystem for years—meaning most of its sea treasures haven't yet been ruined and probably won't be, at least not in the near future. The government has designated the entire area around the island a protected marine park and installed permanent moorings to minimize reef damage.

Diving around the island, actually the peak of an underwater mountain, is excellent, some of the best in the Caribbean, with the best reefs lying within the protected lee of the island. The reefs start as close as twenty yards offshore and the clear waters make visibility excellent, allowing divers to see the abundant coral, mangroves, and more than two hundred species of fish—including parrot fish, queen triggerfish, and spotted moray eels—up to two hundred feet away.

To explore most of the eighty identified dive sites, you can either start from the beaches or from a boat in the sea, beginning in deep water and working your way into the shallow water, essentially decompressing during the second half of the dive. Within the past few years, there's been an increase in the development of snorkeling possibilities, with twelve prime sites now identified. Night dives, too, are becoming increasingly popular.

With year-round temperatures ranging from seventy-eight to eighty-two degrees and only twelve inches of rain a year, chances are good that you'll be able to dive or lounge on the beach every day of a vacation. Bonaire is also outside of the Hurricane Belt, so no weather worries in that respect either.

Although most people come to Bonaire for what's *in* the water, not necessarily what's *next* to the water, the island does sport numerous clean, beautiful, and unusually colored beaches: the black sand of Boca Cocolishi, the pink sand of the aptly named Pink Beach, and the more mainstream white sand of Boca Slagbaai, to name just a few of the best beaches.

Almost all island resorts offer diving and snorkeling packages, and the basics in terms of swimming pools, sea views, and restaurants, but few other amenities. The island itself—sparsely populated with only 11,500 permanent residents—doesn't offer a lot in the way of entertainment, except in the capital of Kralendijk, known locally as "Playa," where there's a small choice of restaurants, bars, and boutiques as well as a casino and disco.

Ambergris Caye

LOCATION: Island of Belize off the Caribbean coast of Central America
HIGH SEASON: November–February LOW SEASON: May–November
CONTACT: Belize Tourism Board, 421 Seventh Avenue, New York, NY 10001; (800) 585-5081, (212) 563-6011; fax: (212) 563-6033
http://www.belize.com

For most visitors, their first view of the 185-mile Barrier Reef, the second longest in the world after Australia's Great Barrier Reef, is from the air: an unbroken chain of white surf running along the Caribbean coast of Mexico's Yucatan Peninsula and down parallel to Belize. On clear days, you can actually see the reef as a narrow yellow line, separating the light blue shallow waters inside the reef from the deep royal blue waters outside.

Diving is possible from many places in Belize, but Ambergris Caye (pronounced "key"), one of two hundred of the islands that dot the Caribbean coast of Belize, remains a favorite for its proximity to some of the best dive sites. Although the island is twenty-five miles long by one mile wide, San Pedro Town is its only town, a friendly and casual place where shorts, T-shirts, and bare feet to walk the sandy streets are the order of the day. At night, divers trade stories to the strains of reggae, salsa, and Spanish and American tunes.

Most of the hotels clustering in town are simple and functional by American standards, while the more luxurious resorts outside of town offer traditional amenities—and better beaches. In San Pedro, the narrow beach is crowded with tourists, boats, and even cargo, becoming wider and more tranquil as you move outside of town. Almost all hotels offer dive packages.

The clear and shallow (about six to eight feet deep) waters inside the reef—only a quarter of a mile from the beach—are populated with friendly dolphins, nurse sharks, and brilliant fish of all colors among the majestic coral gardens. Even snorkeling inside the reef provides more variety than diving in many other sites.

As for diving, there are several good sites within thirty minutes of the caye. One of the most popular dive sites is Hol Chan, at the southern end of the island, a protected marine reserve packed with colorful marine life of all kinds. Other nearby options include Victoria Tunnel, where coral canyons have formed into a long tunnel; Pillar Corals, with coral, sponge, grouper, and smaller fish; and Amigos Wreck, a small barge with nurse sharks. A little farther afield are Turneffe and Lighthouse Reef (with the famous Blue Hole and its huge stalactites), two of Belize's three atolls (of only four in the entire Western Hemisphere).

West End, Roatán

LOCATION: West coast of Roatán, one of the Bay Islands of Honduras, forty miles off the north coast of Honduras
HIGH SEASON: June LOW SEASON: November
CONTACT: Honduras Tourism Office, P.O. Box 140458, Coral Gables, FL 33114; (800) 410-9608, (305) 461-0600; fax: (305) 461-0602
http://www.hondurasinfo.hn

Although just hours away from most North American gateways, Honduras remains fairly isolated from the tourism throngs of other Caribbean destinations, leaving its dive sites in a pristine state, mostly unseen and untouched. Roatán, one of three inhabited islands off the coast of Honduras, is surrounded by reefs offering dazzling coral formations and drop-offs, caverns and delicate fans, and a colorful and exotic profusion of marine life. The island itself is hilly, rugged, and evergreen with the lush jungle; temperatures hover pleasantly in the eighties most of the year with just a hint of a breeze from the trade winds.

Divers head to the west end of the island, where you can just walk to the edge of the palm-fringed beaches and down you go. Drop-offs begin in twenty to forty-five feet of water and visibility ranges from eighty to 150 feet. More than fifty dive sites are within twenty minutes from the shore, where divers can see sixty-five of the sixty-seven known Caribbean corals.

Most of the island's resorts—ranging from clean and simple to unpretentious luxury—are tucked among banana and coconut palms and other fruit trees. They front secluded expanses of white-sand beach and turquoise waters, and because most visitors come to the islands to dive, the majority of hotels feature special dive packages.

Another ocean highlight here is at the Institute of Marine Sciences, where you get the chance to swim with the dolphins. Six to eight people can snorkel and play with the dolphins in a large pen. And for a truly unusual experience, divers can arrange to go out in a boat, get settled at the botton of the sea, and then be joined by a group of dolphins (plus a dive master and dolphin trainer) to experience playing with dolphins in the open water.

Outside of the water, activities tend to the simple: hiking along the mountainous ridge that runs along the center of the island, through tropical trees, pockets of rain forest, vines, and flowers, or along the coast of the island, which ranges from a dramatic iron shore coastline to the beautiful sandy beaches and inlets near the resorts. Be forewarned, though: This is Central America *and* an island. Things get done—eventually. In the meantime, have a second cup of Honduran coffee, settle down on the dock with a freshly picked mango, swing on the hammock with a tropical drink—and relax.

Grand Turk

LOCATION: Island of Turks and Caicos; Atlantic Ocean
HIGH SEASON: December–March LOW SEASON: July–August
CONTACT: Turks and Caicos Islands Tourist Board,
11645 Biscayne Boulevard, Suite 302, Miami, FL 33181;
(800) 241-0824, (305) 891-4117; fax: (305) 891-7096

If the Cayman Islands or Bonaire is too tame for your taste when it comes to activities besides diving, then Grand Turk, one of the eight inhabited islands of Turks and Caicos, isn't the place for you. It's even *more* quiet and low-key, with no glittering nightclubs or casinos, no sprawling resorts, no golf course, frankly not much of anything besides long stretches of almost empty powdery white beaches. On land, that is.

But beneath the water is another story entirely. Only a few hundred yards offshore is Grand Turk's Wall, with a sheer drop that reaches depths of seven thousand feet. You start off easily enough, in waters of forty to fifty feet, and then suddenly that's it—there's seemingly *nothing* below you. You're floating in what looks like an abyss.

Along the face of the cliff are bizarre coral formations, including an area where you can stop and rest for a while, watching the movements of the hawksbill turtles, stingrays, manta rays, and, from December through March, the pods of humpback whales that migrate through the passageways. In addition to the wall, there are several other areas for diving right offshore—sometimes as close as only two to three minutes by boat—including mini-walls covered in hard and soft corals. Coral Gardens is close enough to swim to without a problem, and for night diving, the Library is the place to be with its black coral, orange anemone, and octopi.

The profusion of colors below water contrasts rather sharply with the dry, brownish face of the island. No lush jungle here, just stunted pine, thorny scrub, and cactus. Good beaches run around the perimeter of the island—clean, white, uncluttered with people or buildings, ideal for relaxing and truly getting away from it all.

Limited sightseeing centers in Cockburn Town, the small capital of the colony, where historic homes line the narrow streets. The island's handful of hotels, really more like guest houses or inns since only one has more twenty rooms, are in and around town and are more likely to be called "comfortable" than anything else, although service is typically good. There are few restaurants outside of the hotels, so if you have the option of taking a meal plan, you might as well go for it.

Ghizo Island

LOCATION: Western island of the Solomon Islands, South Pacific
HIGH SEASON: April–December LOW SEASON: January–March
CONTACT: Tourism Council of the South Pacific,
475 Lake Boulevard, P.O. Box 7440, Tahoe City, CA 96145;
(916) 583-0152; fax: (916) 583-0154

If the Solomon Islands just offered its abundance of coral, big fish, and steep drop-offs, it would still be enough to attract most divers. But factor in the wrecks and it becomes an experience unlike any other. These wrecks are real, not intentionally sunk to attract divers as in many other places, and they're not hundreds of years old: They're the mute testimony to the heavy fighting that occurred in this South Pacific region between the Japanese and Allied forces during World War II.

In truth, you could choose almost any of the thirty or so islands for pristine beaches, fascinating island culture, and incredible diving opportunities, but some are a little more developed for divers than others. Around Gizo, the capital of Ghizo Island (different spelling, same pronunciation), is an abundance of fascinating diving sites and adequate, though anything but fancy, lodging possibilities. Although most are in fairly small rest houses, where you pretty much get a bed and a shared bathroom, there are a couple of real hotels, most notably the Gizo Hotel and its upstairs neighbor, the Paradise Lodge.

Just a sampling of natural dive spots near the island includes Grand Central Station, so called for its abundance of colorful coral and crowds of big fish; Supermarket, named because it's well stocked with marine life; Kennedy Wall, a steep drop-off packed with coral and fish; and the Secret Spot, where you can come eye to eye with silvertips.

As for wrecks, the 450-foot Japanese transport ship

Toa Maru still looks ready to sail, filled with sake bottles, gas masks, and even a wok from the kitchen, except, of course, for the fact that it lies on its side in fifty feet of water. Both sides lost fighter planes in the area: The American Hellcat is still intact at about thirty-five feet underwater, as is the Japanese Zero fighter plane, in about fifteen feet of water only a few yards offshore.

There are also several nearby islands within easy boating distance that offer unusual diving opportunities, as well as sightseeing: Skull Island, where you can go back in time to the days of head-hunting (not as far back as you might think—head-hunting was an accepted practice here until the 1920s) and see a shrine composed of the skulls of local chiefs and warriors; Kennedy Island, where JFK and his PT 109 boat crew were stranded for a few days; and Simbo Island, where there are archeological sites, ancient petroglyphs, and the thermal waters of Lake Ove, where villagers cook megapode bird eggs.

7

Back to Nature

The Best Beaches for Ecotourism

Kalalau Beach

LOCATION: Na Pali coast in the northwest of the island of Kauai, Hawaii
HIGH SEASON: November–April LOW SEASON: June–August
CONTACT: Hawaii Visitors and Convention Bureau,
180 Montgomery Street, Suite 2360, San Francisco, CA 94104;
(800) 353-5846, (415) 248-3800; fax: (415) 248-3808
http://www.gohawaii.com

If you're looking for the "real" Hawaii, the mystical remote island nation of lore, Kalalau Beach on the island of Kauai is one of the few places to still find it. It's not easy to get there—in fact, it's downright difficult, but that's been this beach's saving grace. Few tourists have the energy to make the trek to get there or the will to camp in a place with zero modern amenities. (Okay, you *can* take a boat from Hanalei Bay and even leave instructions for it to pick you up again, but hiking down is half the experience.)

Many people get their first (and only) view of this virtually deserted white-sand gem from either a helicopter or a pull-off from Waimea Canyon Drive, where they look down in awe at the knife-edged cliffs and overgrown gorges that drop to the sea four thousand feet below. At the base, the sheer cliffs form a half-circle around Kalalau Beach, with a tall waterfall that ends near the campsite back near the cliffs and then flows into the ocean at the front.

Another waterfall winds through the emerald valleys above to end in a series of rock pools, surrounded by an abundance of tropical fruit ripe for the picking.

The eleven-mile hike from Ke'e Beach on the north shore down to Kalalau Beach is arduous at best and requires a permit, but does give the chance for a breather after two miles at Hanakapiai Beach, a white sandy beach where camping is permitted during the summer but the ocean waters are hazardous, and then another camping option four miles later at Hanakoa Valley, though there's no beach there. The last five miles of the trip are for serious—and well-prepared—hikers only, with precipitous trails, possible landslides, and a stream to cross, but if you can take it, you'll end on the sloping, sandy beach, probably just in time for the spectacular sunset.

Unbelievable as it might seem, native Hawaiians were living in these remote valleys until the early decades of this century, to be replaced in the 1960s by hippies attracted by the valley's isolated beauty and mysterious ancient stone walls and structures. The hippies are gone now, too, but a laissez-faire attitude still prevails on the beach. Want to take your clothes off before wading out to the underwater lava caves and big lava tube just off the shoreline? Go ahead. Prefer to don your bathing suit before washing off in one of the beach's two waterfalls? No problem. Respect for the environment and each other is the keyword here.

Respect for the majesty and power of the ocean is also essential: The surf can be hard and pounding, and do look carefully before venturing in—sharks also gather in the area's remote splendor.

Manuel Antonio

LOCATION: Midway down the Pacific coast of Costa Rica
HIGH SEASON: December–April LOW SEASON: May–November
CONTACT: Costa Rica Tourist Board, P.O. Box 777, San Jose, Costa Rica, 1000; (800) 343-6332
http://www.tourism-costarica.com

In a country where more than a quarter of the land is dedicated to national parks and wildlife refuges, it's not surprising that some of the best beaches have been preserved in their most natural state. The three beaches of Manuel Antonio State Park, just a few miles from the sleepy fishing town of Quepos, are a prime example: pristine white-sand beaches, shaded by leafy trees and fronting the Pacific Ocean, where the people and iguanas (some up to five feet long) sunbathe and swim. Don't be surprised to also share beach space with white-faced monkeys, two-toed sloths, and raccoons, who all occasionally venture out of the lush rain forest behind the beach for a bit of sun.

The park is the most popular in the country for tourists, so sometimes the beaches do get a little crowded; if you want more privacy, head over to the lush cove a few hundred yards away. Another more secluded lagoon hides behind cliffs and rocks—just keep an eye on the tide or you could have a hard time getting back. To get away even more, try an excursion to one of the twelve uninhabited islets just off the coast.

The park is about a three-hour drive from the capital city of San José, so you could do the beach as a daytrip, but then you wouldn't have time for the rest of the park. If you base in Quepos for at least a couple of days, you'll have the time to relax on the beaches and explore the misty green jungle, with its abundance of orchids and other plant life, chattering monkeys, and brightly colored toucans. There are a number of small hotels, villas, and bungalows in Quepos, including the El Parador Hotel and Beach Club, which has recently caught the eye of celebrities such as Martin Sheen and Don Johnson.

Crystal Beach

LOCATION: On Bolivar Peninsula across the Ship Channel from Galveston, Texas

HIGH SEASON: April–September LOW SEASON: October–March

CONTACT: Bolivar Peninsula Chamber of Commerce, P.O. Box 1170, Crystal Beach, TX 77650; (800) 386-7863, (409) 684-5940; fax: (409) 684-5940 http://www.crystalbeach.com

Part of the fun of going to Crystal Beach is taking the public ferry from Galveston Island, crossing the three miles of Houston Ship Channel to Bolivar Peninsula (ferries conveniently depart every fifteen or twenty minutes). Bobbing seagulls always follow the rear of the ferry looking for a handout, and there's a good chance dolphins will play alongside the boat, so bring your binoculars. The sunset crossing is particularly beautiful.

Vacationing on Crystal Beach means lazy days of fishing, crabbing, and shelling. Fishing off the granite rocks of North Jetty is usually good most of the year, with bait and refreshments readily available. Children often play on the nearby beaches or scramble over the rocks to help catch crabs for a fresh seafood feast. Commercial fishing boats harvest shrimp, crabs, and oysters, and their boats are docked at the seafood houses, providing a romantic photo opportunity on summer evenings.

The gulf-side beach on the narrow peninsula is known as "The Flats," a natural nesting ground and feeding area; the ideal place to observe water fowl. During the spring and fall migrations, bird-watchers come from all over the world to enjoy the large numbers of birds stopping to rest and prepare for their journey northward. As an added bonus, the shining wet sands are scattered at certain times of the year with perfectly intact seashells—limpet, sundial, wentletrap, olive, janthia, spiral, tulip shell, rock shell, pen shell, auger, and sand dollars.

There are several hundred beach houses in Crystal Beach available on a weekly basis from individual home owners or numerous real estate companies. The rental units are all privately owned homes with full kitchens and sleeping facilities for families of various sizes. Everything you need is within reach—a variety of fine restaurants, grocery stores, a bank, a water slide, nightclubs, gift shops, and video and convenience stores up and down the peninsula.

Dominica

LOCATION: Eastern Caribbean
HIGH SEASON: January–June LOW SEASON: August–October
CONTACT: Dominica Tourist Office, 820 Second Avenue, New York, NY 10017; (212) 599-8478; fax: (212) 808-4975

First things first: The Caribbean island of Dominica (pronounced "Domineeca") is not the same as the Caribbean island of the Dominican Republic (which actually is half of the same land mass as Haiti). It's packaging itself as the "Nature Island," and the name is apt, especially now when its charms are still relatively undiscovered. Dominica is one of the few Caribbean islands whose major industry is *not* tourism (so far, at least). So you get the chance to really explore a natural wonderland of beaches, rain forests, knife-edge ridges, and the bubbling Boiling Lake without hundreds of other tourists tagging right behind.

If your preference is small, mostly family-run guest houses or hotels that don't have more than forty rooms, you're in luck; if resorts with spas and golf courses are your preference, check back in a decade or so and you might find some. The main town is Roseau on the southwest. Cruises that do call at Dominica stop here, so you don't get quite the away-from-it-all feeling that dominates on the other parts of the island; on the other hand, you have a better choice of hotels and restaurants.

Although the beach might be part of a Dominica vacation, it is, in truth, not the highlight. Many of the beaches on the Caribbean side of the island were washed away in 1995, but the black-sand beaches are slowly returning. For now, though, the most beautiful, quiet, and unspoiled beaches are on the northeast coast, especially Pointe Baptiste, a private nature reserve where there are black and white sand beaches, coastal forest, and a headland of sculptured red rock. It fronts the Atlantic Ocean, where swimming conditions can sometimes be dangerous because of large underswells and occasional freak waves. The closest town is Portsmouth, a popular stopping point for yachts in the area, with several small hotels, guest houses, and cottages.

The diving around Dominica has been hailed as some of the best, and least disturbed, in the Caribbean. The area is also the best in the region for whale watching, because the mothers and young stay in the Caribbean waters for most of the year. It's not unusual for them to swim near the boats, with young males making enormous jumps before diving below the waves. If the whales don't come nearby, you can surely count on a school of dolphin to accompany your boat, especially near Soufriere Bay, also popular for diving.

The interior of the island is spectacular for hiking through the tropical green rain forest, particularly the Valley of Desolation, an area of sulfur springs and boiling water made of multicolored minerals left in the water from old volcanic activity. At the end of the trail (at least three or four hours hiking) is Boiling Lake, the largest of its kind in the world, kept constantly bubbling from the volcanic heat that comes from its crater.

Cannon Beach

LOCATION: Fifty miles northeast of Portland, OR
HIGH SEASON: June–October LOW SEASON: November–April
CONTACT: Cannon Beach Chamber of Commerce, P.O. Box 64, Cannon Beach, Oregon 97110; (503) 436-2623; fax: (503) 436-0910

Nine miles of walkable Cannon Beach offers a romantic, ever-changing view of the "seastacks" in the ocean and the headlands on shore. Have your binoculars ready to train on the variety of whales that pass close to the beach during winter and spring, as well as the birds that swirl over famous Haystack Rock, at 235 feet high the third largest coastal monolith in the world. Haystack Rock is designated as a marine and bird sanctuary, and many live sea creatures live in the tidepools around it. It's like visiting a natural Seaworld—you can pick up limpets, barnacles, starfish, crabs, sea sculpins, and anemones. Several bird species nest on the rock in the summer, the most colorful the tufted puffin with its white face, orange bill, and a tuft of feathers above the eyes.

Nature-lovers will enjoy Cannon Beach's many trails, with inspiring names like Cape Falcon Trail, Saddle Mountain Trail, and the Neahkahnie Mountain Summit trail. For the less active, there are lots of easy paths through the thick conifer forests of Ecola State Park, leading from the beach up to viewpoints and picnic areas overlooking the panorama of Cannon Beach and the Coast Range. In Klootchy Creek Park, you can see the world's tallest Sitka spruce, located in an old-growth fir and spruce forest just a few miles from Cannon Beach. The spruce, at 216 feet high with a trunk circumference of fifty-two feet, is an incredible seven centuries old.

Strolling is the preferred mode of transportation in town, where you can find some of the best crafts, art galleries, and bistros on the coast. Others prefer bicycling or horseback riding, and you can even rent three-wheel tricycles for a relaxing glide down to the beach or through the wooded hillsides.

In this out-of-the-way place, lodgings include inns, motels, resorts, and condominium rentals. Many of the rooms have spectacular views of the ocean and direct access to the beach.

Hulopoe Beach

LOCATION: South coast of Lanai, Hawaii
HIGH SEASON: November–April LOW SEASON: June–August
CONTACT: Hawaii Visitors and Convention Bureau,
180 Montgomery Street, Suite 2360, San Francisco, CA 94104;
(800) 353-5846, (415) 248-3800; fax: (415) 248-3808
http://www.gohawaii.com

Who says ecotourism and luxury can't coexist? In the early 1990s, they took a stab at it on Lanai and, so far, it's working well. The very embodiment of the merger between the two comes at Hulopoe Beach in Lanai, where the newer of two of the island's resorts, the Manele Bay Hotel, overlooks Hulopoe Bay from a spot atop the bluff. The hotel is a classic upscale beach resort, a Mediterranean-style complex complete with tropical gardens, a golf course, and beach views from each of the 250 lavishly furnished guest rooms. (The other island resort is the Lodge at Koele, a low-rise resort with a decidedly English manor feel, set among tall pine trees in the cooler hills seven miles away.)

The beach at Hulopoe is the island's only accessible white-sand beach. It's a beauty, a broad quarter-mile expanse of white sand that forms a crescent around the gentle waves, excellent for swimming, snorkeling, diving, and even surfing. To the east, just around the bend in the shoreline, are tidal pools where kids play. Round another corner and Sweetheart Rock rises in front of a pretty little cove.

The beach was a site for locals long before the hotel opened, and it remains public, hosting a fairly easy mix of wealthy tourists and Lanai residents—not to mention the porpoises, although they don't come as close to shore as they used to. As for the residents, there are only about three thousand of them, living in Lanai City, a picturesque town originally developed by the Dole Pineapple Company in the 1920s when the entire island was devoted to the pineapple industry. The majority of the island is still privately owned, and the decision to develop limited tourism was made when it became cheaper to grow pineapple elsewhere.

The best way to get around the island is to rent a four-wheel-drive. Only thirty miles of paved roads cover the little island (thirteen by eighteen miles); the rest are unpaved roads and Jeep trails. You can either take a four-wheel-drive or hike up the twelve-mile Munroe Trail, where the view on a clear day encompasses the whole island plus all the other major islands in the Hawaiian chain. Other highlights are the Garden of the Gods, where eerie rock formations change colors at dawn and dusk, and Shipwreck Beach, where the rust-colored sand is littered with the fragments of ships that couldn't make it and a World War II ship is grounded just off the shoreline.

Grand Anse

LOCATION: Southwestern tip of island of Grenada, Caribbean
HIGH SEASON: December–March, July–August
LOW SEASON: April–June, September–November
CONTACT: Grenada Board of Tourism, 820 Second Avenue, Suite 900D, New York, NY 10017; (800) 927-9554, (212) 687-9554; fax: (212) 573-9731
http://www.interknowledge.com/grenada

Sometimes it takes folks a minute or two to remember why the name "Grenada" sounds so familiar: Is it the beaches they've heard of? The nightlife? The rain forest? Most times, it comes back slowly—oh yes, that was that island we "invaded" in the early eighties to "save" from Communism. Without going into the complicated politics of the situation, suffice it to say that the government of Grenada (comprising three islands, the largest of which is also called Grenada) is now a democracy and quite safe for travelers.

Unlike many Caribbean islands, its main industry is agriculture, not tourism, which means that although some parts of the island have been developed for tourism, many others remain real places where real people live and work—a refreshing change in the tourism-dominated Caribbean. Roads are narrow, twisty, and hilly, passing by farms and plantations and large undeveloped areas of rain forests, beaches, mountains, and waterfalls.

The greatest concentration of hotels is along the Grand Anse beach, but it's the white-sand beach and blue waters that dominate the view here, not the hotels, since none is allowed to be taller than the coco palms that also line the two-mile beach. A smooth expanse of beach that stretches around the gentle curve of a bay, Grand Anse does occasionally get crowded with cruise passengers in for the day from the nearby capital of St. George's, but there's usually plenty of room for everyone. For a little more privacy, the pleasant bay and beach at Morne Rouge is just a few minutes away.

Whatever other sightseeing you choose to do, make sure you leave Saturday morning open for the outdoor markets in St. George's, where the subtle aromas of nutmeg, cinnamon, and vanilla wafting through the colorful stands are a fragrant reminder of why the island is usually referred to as "Spice Island." (Bring some home, but make sure it's prepackaged so there are no Customs problems.)

Outside of the beach and capital, sightseeing runs to natural pleasures, especially hiking and trekking the rain forest of Grand Etang Forest Reserve, just a short drive from the coast but another world, high up in the mountains of the island's interior. The focal point is the azure waters of Grand Etang Lake, which fills the crater of one of the island's extinct volcanoes and is home to a rich diversity of colorful tropical birds, tiny lizards, and rare orchids. Also in the south, La Sagesse Nature Center, a quiet mangrove estuary great for bird-watching, has three fine beaches edged with palm trees and good coral reef for snorkeling.

Block Island

LOCATION: Twelve miles off the southern coast of Rhode Island
HIGH SEASON: July–Labor Day LOW SEASON: November–April
CONTACT: Block Island Chamber of Commerce, Drawer D, Block Island, RI 02807; (800) 383-2474, (401) 466-2982; fax: (401) 466-5286
http://www.blockisland.com

You might expect that tourists would be flocking to (and ruining) the island called one of the "twelve last great places in the Western hemisphere" by the Nature Conservancy. To be sure, there are plenty of day-trippers who do take the one-hour ferry ride over to the little island, but they mostly stay on one beach, leaving the rest of the unspoiled island one of the most uncrowded (and inexpensive) in the Northeast.

Rugged bluffs, a rolling green landscape, salt ponds, and miles of sandy beaches are what earned the island that designation and set the scene for old-fashioned, unsophisticated beach vacationing where sunbathing, swimming, shell collecting, sailing, and nature hikes are the order of the day. The whole island is only seven miles long and three miles wide with walkable, if not all swimmable, beaches creating a loop around an interior of wide open spaces and two quiet towns, Old Harbor and New Harbor, the second being more a small grouping of facilities than an actual town. Since it's just as easy to walk or bike (on rented bicycles) around the island as to drive, most visitors choose to leave their cars on the mainland.

The best island beaches for swimming run along a two-mile string on the east side, collectively named Crescent Beach: Just north of the harbor, Fred Benson Town Beach (also called State Beach) is the most crowded with day-trippers, but also the only one to have public facilities, such as restrooms and changing areas, vendors, and snack bars, as well as lifeguards. To its north, Scotch Beach is most popular with teenagers and college students, while farther north is the pretty Mansion Beach, with the rugged bluffs in the distance and a sandy ocean bottom that remains shallow a ways out.

The south side is for the hardier, with both surf and seclusion in most places, except near the 150 wooden steps that lead up to the Southeast Lighthouse, the highest lighthouse in New England, and a popular tourist spot. The beaches to the west and north are pleasant for walking and cookouts, but not for swimming, especially in the north, where the currents are dangerous.

Block Island's accommodations are in keeping with its relaxed atmosphere, mostly big wooden Victorian hotels (check carefully before booking—some have been spruced up but others haven't) and smaller inns and bed-and-breakfasts. There's no camping on the island.

Marco Island

LOCATION: Island off southwest tip of Florida
HIGH SEASON: December–April LOW SEASON: June–August
CONTACT: Marco Island and the Everglades Convention and Visitors Bureau, 1102 North Collier Boulevard, Marco Island, FL 34145; (800) 788-MARCO, (941) 394-7549; fax: (941) 394-3061 http://www.marco-island-florida.com

As the largest of Florida's Ten Thousand Islands, Marco Island is also the only inhabited island of the group. Known both as a gateway to the Everglades and as a destination in its own right, the island offers that rare combination of upscale resorts and amenities (along with mid-range hotels) and unspoiled nature. Families or couples looking for a safe and quiet getaway find it in the large clean beaches that front the calm and warm waters of the Gulf of Mexico.

Unlike many other Florida beaches, these are not crowded or eroded, and the hotels are quite reasonably priced compared to other upper-end hotels. Because airport access is a little difficult (the nearest airport is the Southwest Florida International Airport fifty miles away in Fort Myers, but most come in through the Miami Airport), many hotels bundle rental cars in their packages. The drive from Miami takes about two hours, with eighty miles through the treasures of the Everglades National Park, so the sightseeing end of your vacation can actually start before you even reach the island.

With an easy pace and casual atmosphere, the island is best suited to somewhat quiet pursuits—shelling for clams, cockles, conch shells, and even starfish and

Florida sand dollars; fishing for snook, red fish, tarpon, king mackerel, and grouper; taking a boat out to explore any of the area's uninhabited islands or the Everglades' River of Grass by canoe, airboat, or kayak. By car, the Everglades is only half an hour away, well worth the trip to visit the largest subtropical wilderness in the United States, with its extraordinary variety of wildlife, including alligators, the only salt-water crocodiles in the United States, pelicans, and even black bears.

The island itself sports large areas of wilderness, along with private coves and natural lagoons ideal for truly getting away from it all. It's these very hiding spots that long attracted pirates and explorers, some of whom are memorialized now. The area is also home to thirty-nine golf courses, many top-tier ones designed by the pros.

Vieques Island

LOCATION: Seven miles east of main island of Puerto Rico, United States
HIGH SEASON: November–April LOW SEASON: July–October
CONTACT: Puerto Rico Tourism Company, 575 Fifth Avenue, New York, NY 10017; (800) 223-6530, (212) 599-6262; fax: (212) 818-1866
http://www.discoverpuertorico.com

While San Juan is definitely the sightseeing and cultural capital of Puerto Rico (with its own assortment of beaches), Vieques Island offers an old-fashioned Caribbean charm, with coral reefs, horses that roam freely, mangrove lagoons that attract more than a hundred kinds of birds, and some fifty virtually empty beaches.

The palm-lined beaches run around the perimeter, and although some sport colorful nicknames like Green Beach, Blue Beach, and Red Beach, most remain anonymous stretches of pure white sand. The little fishing village of Esperanza, on the south side, is home to most of the island's hotels and one of the island's most crowded beaches, Sun Bay, a little crescent of white sand with public facilities, including a bathhouse and picnic tables.

The casinos of San Juan never made it out to this island, but you can still experience an incredible sound and light show at night listening to the *coquis,* tiny chirping tree frogs, and watching the waters of Phosphorescent Bay (Mosquito Bay) come alive with light. The waters are inhabited by rare organisms that glow neon when agitated by the movement of a boat or even a hand in the water. Jump into the water and watch the luminescent trails shoot as you move parts of your body.

The island is only about seven miles off the east coast Puerto Rico and accessible either by plane from San Juan or by ferry from Fajardo, where there are beaches and a handful of low-budget accommodations. Even if you choose not to stay there, try to get a look at the nearby El Conquistador Resort, the largest self-contained resort in the United States.

Just inland from Fajardo starts El Yunque, a real rain forest (it's almost a guarantee that you will be rained on, if only briefly, if you spend more than an hour or so there), with twenty-eight thousand acres crisscrossed with hiking trails that offer glimpses of the colorful Puerto Rican parrot, the occasional boa, and seemingly endless greenery.

8

On the Road

The Best Beaches for Sightseeing

Nice

LOCATION: Southeast France
HIGH SEASON: July–August LOW SEASON: October
CONTACT: French Government Tourist Office,
444 Madison Avenue, 16th floor, New York, NY 10022;
(900) 990-0040 ($.50/minute); fax: (212) 838-7855
http://www.francetourism.com

The French Riviera: It's Nice. At least that's what the T-shirts proclaim, and they're not far off. Nice might not have all the glamour of some of the other Côte d'Azur cities, or all the charm of the little medieval villages that perch atop the mountains lining the coast, but it does make a great base for exploring those areas. And, as the second most popular tourist city in France (following Paris, of course), it has a significantly larger concentration of all levels of hotels, restaurants, and stores than any of the other cities on the Riviera, plus its own international airport with some direct flights from the United States.

It's a strange situation for an area that's become renowned worldwide as a beach destination, but the truth is, the beaches here are mostly small, and almost all of them are lined with pebbles, not sand. Ever trying lying on a towel on top of a layer of pebbles? Not fun. Fortunately, most of the tourist areas rent out chairs, but even walking and getting in and out of the ocean has its challenges.

Women: If you don't want to look American, take off the top of your bathing suit and wear a just-barely-there bottom. Men: If you don't want to look American, dig up the tiniest Speedo you can find and then buy it at least one size too small. This is, after all, the Riviera.

Nice itself offers much more than the beach, including a quaint Old Town, with an exquisite flower market; Cimiez, Roman ruins at the edge of town; numerous museums, including one dedicated to Chagall and one to Matisse; and shopping to rival that of Paris. The most prestigious hotels line the paved Promenade des Anglais, a wide walkway that parallels the ocean. The most opulent among them is the Hotel Negresco, well worth a look even though it's way out of the price range for most of us.

Daytrips out of the city could keep you busy for days: Grasse, where perfume is made and you can get great deals on famous brand-name perfumes in generic bottles; Biot, home of bubbled glass; Eze, a medieval village atop a mountain with cobblestone streets and buildings too quaint for words; and Villefranche-sur-Mer, a medieval harbor town with brightly colored buildings and steep narrow streets.

Crete

LOCATION: Aegean Islands, Greece
HIGH SEASON: May–September LOW SEASON: October–April
CONTACT: Greece National Tourist Office, 645 Fifth Avenue,

New York, NY 10022; (212) 421-5777; fax: (212) 826-6940
http://www.compulink.gr/tourism

The largest island in Greece, and the fifth largest in the Mediterranean, Crete is an oblong island characterized by a succession of high mountains, fertile valleys, crowded cities, and picturesque villages. A link between Asia, Africa, and Europe, Crete's unique geographical position made it a center of cultural currents and conflicts that influenced the course of antiquity.

Today the island's most developed beach resorts line the north shore, fronting on the Sea of Crete, with some of the most modern and luxurious hotels in Southern Europe as well as a brisk tourist turnover. The most popular beaches are at Aghios Nikólaos, an international hot spot with a rocky coastline and a charming harbor; the crowded sand beaches of Réthimnon, accented with Turkish minarets, a Venetian fort, and nonstop nightlife; and those outside of Heraklion, the capital of the island and the site of one of the best-known archeological sites in all the world: the ruins of the ancient palace of Knossos.

One of the earliest great civilizations in Europe, the Minoans thrived some four thousand years ago, but they live on today in the stories of Greek mythology. The palace, built around 2000 B.C., was destroyed in 1700 B.C., then rebuilt even more magnificently and destroyed again circa 1500 B.C., most likely from the huge eruption of the volcano on Santorini. The centerpiece of the site is a reconstruction of the palace in all its grandeur while the ancient remains extend for miles around. In the town of Heraklion proper is the Archeology Museum, with more Minoan artifacts than anywhere else in the world.

Exploring Crete can take as much time as you want to give to it. For the basics, you need at least four days;

to do the whole island could easily take weeks. Highlights include the Turkish- and Venetian-flavored Hania on the north; the unspoiled coastline of the Rhodopou Peninsula in the northwest, complete with Christian religious sites and miles of hiking paths; and the more remote beaches and villages in the south and east, where tourists rarely venture high upon the clifftops and deep into the caves.

Stanley Bay

LOCATION: Seaward side of Hong Kong Island
HIGH SEASON: May–September LOW SEASON: October–April
CONTACT: Hong Kong Tourist Association, 590 Fifth Avenue, New York, NY 10036; (212) 840-1690; fax: (212) 730-2605 http://www.hkta.org

Stanley, one of Hong Kong Island's oldest settlements, is picturesquely nestled on the cliffside overlooking the sandbar of Stanley Peninsula. The southeast of Hong Kong Island has remained virtually untouched by land reclamation and is a dramatic mixture of rocky inlets, shady beaches, and some major visitor attractions. You won't find lodging in Stanley itself, but Hong Kong boasts one of the most comprehensive selections of fine accommodations in the world.

The ancient village of Stanley is now a brash, entrepreneurial microcosm of the towering Chinese cities, yet a quiet walk on the beach overlooking picturesque East Lamma Channel evokes a far more ancient world. The old fishing village clings to the steep hillside much as it did in 1934, when the British cut a road to Stanley to combat the pirates and their smuggling activities. Pirates had even taken over the Tin Hau temple, which dates back to 1767, the oldest temple site on Hong Kong Island. To the right of the altar, you can see the temple drum and bell; legend says they belonged to the infamous pirate Cheung Po-tsai, who used Stanley as his lookout post between raids.

Today, the main attraction of this tiny village is the market, which sells silk, linen, sportswear, and curios. This famous alley is about six hundred feet long, barely the size of two tennis courts, but it runs twelve hours a day, seven days a week. In the labyrinth of shops and stalls, among the inexpensive Chinese labels, you can find designer and costly clothing at bargain prices. The best buys are buried among the racks by the wily vendors to keep the mystique and reputation of the marketplace alive. Before 1997 when the Chinese took back Hong Kong, the true worth of Stanley could be judged by the number of expatriate wives of British officials who regularly visited the market to find designer jewels.

Newport

LOCATION: Southern Rhode Island

HIGH SEASON: June–August LOW SEASON: September–May

CONTACT: The Newport County Convention and Visitors Bureau, 23 America's Cup Avenue, Newport, RI 02840: (401) 849-8048 http://www.visitrhodeisland.com/newport.html

Called "America's First Resort," Newport is one of the most historically intact cities in North America; a veritable treasure-trove of landmark buildings. You can take an educational walking tour highlighting history and architecture, or simply stroll along the breathtaking Ocean Drive and the renowned Cliff Walk, discovering secret gardens and hidden colonial graveyards.

Newport began in 1639 when a small group of settlers landed on the southern tip of Aquidneck Island. The area quickly became known as the "Eden of America" because of the protected harbor, rich farmland, and gentle climate. By the eighteenth century, Newport was one of the most thriving seaports in America. Called "American Bath" before the Civil War and "Queen of Resorts" in the Victorian era, Newport became a haven for the wealthy, who provided an important source of patronage for America's leading architects, decorators, and craftsmen. The summer mansions and lavish gardens were commissioned by a "Who's Who" of American wealth and society: Chateau-sur-Mer (1851–52) was built by the China Trade merchant William Shepard Wetmore; Mrs. William K. Vanderbilt commissioned the Marble House (1890s); and the Breakers was quickly erected for Cornelius Vanderbilt II in 1893.

With this much cultural history, Newport has long been synonymous with the arts and music. There are plenty of major festivities in the summer, including the Ben & Jerry's Newport Folk Festival, the Newport Strawberry Festival, and the JVC Jazz Festival. Families seem to gravitate toward the many exhibits at social societies and museums of history, science, naval heritage, and yachting.

Renowned for its fresh seafood, Newport offers romantic dinners for two by candlelight with a harbor view, or a family meal for you and the kids for under $20. Accommodations range from standard hotels to unique lodgings in elegant Victorian houses near the beach. You can even stay in the restored, century-old lighthouse on Rose Island, which is both a museum and two-room bed-and-breakfast.

Kuşadasi

LOCATION: Aegean coast of Turkey
HIGH SEASON: May–September LOW SEASON: October–April
CONTACT: Turkish Government Tourist Office,
821 United Nations Plaza, New York, NY 10017;
(212) 687-2194; fax: (212) 599-7568
http://www.turkey.org/turkey

Built along the shores of a glittering bay around a tiny flower-covered islet, the terraced town of Kuşadasi overlooks the Aegean Sea just south of the midpoint along the Turkish coastline. Called "Bird Island," the port town has long been a port of call for cruises, and with the recent "discovery" of Turkey (in part because of still phenomenally good prices), it has been transformed into a full-fledged resort town, albeit one that retains a good deal of its historical charm.

The beach in town is adequate, but most of the newer hotel complexes line Kadinlar, also called "Ladies' Beach," a half-mile stretch of fine-powder-sand beaches about two miles from the harbor where a wide promenade separates the sea from the main avenue and provides the bulk of entertainment options. Up and down the coast from Kuşadasi, other popular beach resort towns within easy driving distance include the fishing village and former pirate stronghold of Foça; the ancient city of Bodrum, transformed into one of the liveliest of the Aegean resorts; and the palm-lined Marmaris, where the Aegean meets the Mediterranean. Although the Aegean is booming, it's still quite easy to stumble onto uncrowded beaches along the coast, where tourism hasn't yet infiltrated.

Kuşadasi itself offers a maze of winding streets in a picturesque old quarter and a fifteenth-century fortress said to have been a favorite among pirates, but some of the best sightseeing in all the world is within about an hour's drive. About a half hour by car, the two-thousand-year-old marble streets, huge theater, and renowned library of Ephesus stand as mute testimony to the glory of ancient Roman Asia Minor. Nearby, a single column is the only remainder of the Temple of Artemis, one of the Seven Wonders of the Ancient World.

Farther inland, there's Pamukkale. Its name means "cotton castles," an apt description of the astounding cotton-white curtain of stalagmites and stepped shallow pools that form an otherworldly landscape. On the way south from Pamukkale to Aphrodisias, a city dedicated to the worship of the goddess of love Aphrodite, stop at the Roman ruins, complete with baths and temples of Hieropolis.

Less than an hour north of Kuşadasi, outside of Izmir, is a stone house said to have been the final home of the Virgin Mary, while another hour north, Pergamum was considered one of the most beautiful of the ancient Greek cities.

Carmel-by-the-Sea

LOCATION: Central California, just south of Monterey Bay
HIGH SEASON: March–October LOW SEASON: November–January
CONTACT: Carmel Business/Tourist Information Association,
P.O. Box 4444; Carmel-by-the-Sea, CA 93921;
(408) 624-2522; fax: (408) 624-1329

Nestled in a pine forest above the spectacular white-sand beach below, the one-square-mile village of Carmel has been a haven for artists, writers, and other Bohemian types since its very inception. With tree-lined streets and stuccoed houses with Spanish-tiled roofs, the quaint town brings a bit of the Mediterranean to California. Although tourism is big here, the quirky little town refuses to bend: Streets still have no addresses, and locations are described as north or south of Ocean Avenue and on the east or west side of the street (a hint: west is always towards the ocean). There are numerous shops and galleries throughout the town, but look carefully because many are hidden in courtyards.

Carmel's approximately one thousand guest rooms can be found in resorts, inns, and bed-and-breakfasts. Although it's best to make reservations, the town makes it easy on hapless tourists who wander in: As long as there's a vacancy anywhere in town, a VACANT sign remains on all inns, with a "host of the day" keeping track of where vacancies remain.

Unlike the beaches to the south where the waters are warmer, here only the hardiest swimmers attempt the Pacific that laps onto the beach—it remains a pretty constant fifty-five degrees year-round. Still, the beach has zero development and is a great place for kicking back to grab some rays and then watching the sunset at the end of the day.

Although Carmel's low-key attractions could keep you content for quite a time, nearby Monterey beckons with its renowned aquarium and Cannery Row. And then there's Big Sur. Start on U.S. Route 1 south of Carmel for one of the most spectacular drives in the country, as the two-lane road winds its way along the coast with five-thousand-foot mountains on one side and a steep drop down to the Pacific on the other (not for queasy drivers). At the end of the ninety-mile stretch of coastline is Hearst Castle in San Simeon, a true castle built to fulfill every whim of its eccentric millionaire owner, William Randolph Hearst.

Portland

LOCATION: Southeastern coast of Maine
HIGH SEASON: June–August LOW SEASON: September–May
CONTACT: Convention and Visitors Bureau of Greater Portland,
305 Commercial Street, Portland, ME 04101;
(207) 772-5800; fax: (207) 874-9043
http://www.visitportland.com

Sitting on a peninsula in spectacular Casco Bay, Portland is a place of scenic beauty and splendid recreational opportunities. A variety of countryside and coastal landscapes within a fifteen-mile radius of the city makes for a refreshing getaway. For vacationers who just want to relax, there's always sunbathing on

Portland's warm, sandy beaches or sailing the Atlantic, past the pristine landscape of the Calendar Islands. You can also visit cultural and historic sites in this northern New England town, the largest in Maine, including the Portland Headlight, one of the oldest lighthouses in the United States, commissioned by George Washington in 1791, and the Portland Observatory, constructed in 1807 as a signal tower reporting the approach of ships.

A key to the city's charm lies in its hundred miles of nature and walking trails, some winding through Back Cove and the Eastern Promenade with spectacular views over the Atlantic, which have historically, and rightly, been known as the "Emerald Necklace." Outdoor enthusiasts will find some of the nation's finest scenic and recreational opportunities here, from whitewater rafting to deep-sea or freshwater fishing, downhill or nordic skiing, golfing, sailing, mountain climbing, and bicycling. In all, the area boasts 11 public golf courses, 124 tennis courts, and 95 playgrounds.

Portland has the cultural activities of a major metropolitan area while maintaining a quaint, small-town flavor. Accommodations can be easily found near the Downtown Arts District, where northern New England's abundance of arts and entertainment attractions are concentrated. Best of all, you can enjoy a narrated bus tour or do your own self-guided walking tour of historic Portland neighborhoods on Congress Street, the Old Port Exchange, State Street, and the Western Promenade—all while you browse for antiques before sitting down to a fabulous lobster feast.

Tel Aviv

LOCATION: West coast of Israel
HIGH SEASON: April–September, December
LOW SEASON: January–March
CONTACT: Israel Government Tourist Office,

800 Second Avenue, New York, NY 10017;
(888) 77 ISRAEL, (212) 499-5660; fax: (212) 499-5665
http://www.goisrael.com

Cosmopolitan, commercial, and very modern, Tel Aviv doesn't match the preconceived notion most visitors have of Israel. Where are the ruins? Where are the religious sites? Where are the terrorists? Fortunately, the first two are within easy driving distances of the city, while the last don't show up even a fraction of how often American television would lead us to believe.

The wide tan beaches of Tel Aviv—running for about four miles along the café- and boutique-lined concrete Promenade—are some of the cleanest in the world and attract a healthy mix of tourists and foreign businesspeople, grandparents and toddlers, and tanned young Israeli men and women, arguably among the best-looking people in the world. Most of Tel Aviv's best hotels front the beach, starting near the center of Tel Aviv and getting more expensive and exclusive as they march northward. Gordon Beach, at the Dan Hotel, is one of the most popular, as is Orange Beach at the Hilton. While Tel Aviv is almost aggressively secular, at Nordau Beach, north of the Hilton, religious men and women still divide into separate sections.

Within the city, highlights include the Diaspora Museum, the Tel Aviv Museum of Art, the shopping area of Dizengoff, and the biblical city of Jaffa, essentially merged into Tel Aviv. Nightlife can be hot and frantic or leisurely hours spent at the numerous cafés.

Still, you don't go to Israel simply for the beach. Jerusalem is only about thirty miles away, another world high atop a hill where the ancient winding streets remain a religious center for Jews, Christians, and Muslims. You could easily spend days taking in the major sites there, including the Western (Wailing) Wall, the Church of the Holy Sepulcher, the Temple Mount and Dome of the Rock. Yad Vashem, the most complete museum and memorial to the horror of the Holocaust, includes the touching and horrifying Children's Memorial, where minuscule pinpoints of light cast an eerie glow to accompany the endless recitation of the names, ages, and countries of origin of the 1.5 million children murdered.

It's not until you're in Israel that you realize how truly tiny the country is, a negative in terms of its security within the world, but a plus in terms of sightseeing. Within about an hour of Tel Aviv are the wonders of the Dead Sea (see chapter 10) as well as the historical Masada to the south, and Nazareth, the Crusader city Akko, and the Sea of Galilee to the north. Ancient excavated ruins from biblical and Roman times dot the countryside in all directions.

Playa del Carmen

LOCATION: Southeast coast of Mexico
HIGH SEASON: December–March LOW SEASON: June–August
CONTACT: Mexican Government Tourism Office,
405 Park Avenue, Suite 1401, New York, NY 10022;
(800) 44-MEXICO, (212) 421-6655, (212) 838-2949;
fax: (212) 753-2874
http://mexico-travel.com

About forty miles south of Cancún, along the center of what's now called the Cancún-Tulum Corridor, the new resort area of Playacar is springing up around Playa del Carmen, the port from which the Mayans used to set sail for the sacred island of Cozumel (see chapter 6). Once a lazy little village, Playa del Carmen is now the center of glitzy new resorts that offer the best of both worlds: luxury hotels along the lines of those in Cancún (see chapter 2) that front still-uncrowded white-sand beaches. Plus, for sightseeing, Playa del Carmen is even closer to the Mayan ruins of the Yucatán Peninsula.

The area now supports about thirty-five hotels, with the best lining the beaches, and more are in the works, so it's hard to tell how long the laid-back atmosphere will remain. In the meantime, prices remain better than in Cancún, and there's more a feeling of being in Mexico rather than simply being in a resort. Not to mention the warm, pristine waters that cover small reefs good for snorkeling and diving.

The resort area is close enough to several major attractions to be a good base for daytrips. The closest, only five minutes away, is Xcaret (pronounced "Sh-car-et"), an eco-archeological park the size of Epcot Center where you can swim the two-thousand-foot underground river, explore small Mayan ruins, hang out on the beach by the breathtaking blue lagoon, and, if you get there early enough, sign up to swim with the dolphins. Another thirty miles down the coast is Xel-Ha (pronounced "Shell-ha"), where the interconnected lagoons cut out of the limestone shoreline are home to numerous fish and underwater caves.

From there, it's just another couple of miles to the ruins of the walled city of Tulum, the largest Mayan city on the coast, where you can explore the ruins and climb down to swim off the beach below where ancient boats used to dock. Another half an hour inland, the largely unexcavated ruins of Cobá in the jungle give you a feel for what early archeologists found at all the sites.

The highlight of any Mayan sightseeing, however, is the majestic Chichén Itzá, a two- to three-hour drive from Playa del Carmen. You can easily spend a full day or more exploring the various buildings, including the observatory, where the Mayans refined the science of astronomy to the point where it's only two-ten-thousandths of a day off from the calendar we use today, and the 365-step Temple of Kulkulkan, where the light hits in such a way that a serpent appears to slither down its side during the spring and fall equinoxes. At night a sound and light show actually provides a clearer view than during the day, with narration to go along with it.

Deauville

LOCATION: Normandy; northwest France
HIGH SEASON: July–August LOW SEASON: November–March
CONTACT: French Government Tourist Office,
444 Madison Avenue, 16th floor, New York, NY 10022;
(900) 990-0040 ($.50/minute); fax: (212) 838-7855
http://www.francetourism.com

A planned beach resort since the nineteenth century, Deauville remains a hotbed of social activity for the obviously well-heeled; even if their names might not be familiar to most of us, one look tells the story of titles and servants, designer clothing, and summer and winter palaces. A broad boardwalk overlooks the beach, an expanse of soft gold sand dotted with brightly colored parasols, while inland along the wide avenues are top-drawer hotels, villas, and an upscale casino. The town also sports two race tracks, a yachting harbor, and polo grounds. A stone's throw away is the sister town of Trouville, an older, slightly worn version of Deauville, no longer quite as sophisticated or expensive, but its beach is still lined with magnificent nineteenth-century villas, and the casino can still pack them in.

While both front beautiful stretches of beach and offer all the high-end dining, nightlife, and shopping you could desire, their main attraction for Americans is as a base for excursions along the coast of Normandy. The names of the beaches to the south are familiar to anyone with even the most rudimentary knowledge of American history—Sword, Juno, Gold, Omaha, and Utah, where the Allied forces landed on D-Day in 1944. Although swarms of veterans, their families, history buffs, and others interested in those historic events make their way to pay homage at the big, windswept beaches, they're typically not crowded because they're spread out over large expanses.

Stop in at the Musée du Débarquement to refresh your memory of the events leading up to the historic day, then make your way along the bits of shrapnel and crumbling bunkers that can still be found on the beaches to the American Cemetery. If you need a break along the way, in most places you can just pull out a towel and refresh with some sunbathing and swimming.

While you're in the area, take a brief detour inland to Bayeux, site of the famous tapestry that tells the story of the Battle of Hastings and William the Conqueror's conquest of England in 1066. Then continue southwest to Mont-Saint-Michel, the stunning Gothic abbey and village that rises from the sea on a rocky outcrop. A causeway leads out to it now, but for most of its history since the eighth century, the only way to get there was to cross the bay, risking drownings at high tide and getting sucked under by quicksand.

East from Deauville are several other attractions, including the city of Rouen, with the square where Joan of Arc was burned at the stake and the cathedral painted so many times by Monet; south of Rouen is Giverny, where a Monet museum is set among the gardens of water lilies that he immortalized in painting after painting.

9

Star Gazing

The Best Beaches for Glamour

South Beach

LOCATION: Miami, Florida
HIGH SEASON: December–March LOW SEASON: May–September
CONTACT: Greater Miami Convention and Visitors Bureau,
701 Brickell Avenue, Suite 2700, Miami, FL 33131;
(800) 283-2707, (305) 539-3000, (305) 666-SOBE (Hotline);
fax: (305) 539-3113
http://www.miamiandbeaches.com

If you think of Miami as the place for retired grandparents, think again, at least when it comes to South Beach. Less than two square miles at the bottom of Miami Beach, South Beach has exploded in the past decade, becoming the place to see and be seen in the United States. Only about thirty thousand people live there, but millions visit each year, primarily to gawk at an impressive roster of movie stars, recording artists, and the seemingly nonstop parade of gorgeous fashion models. The ambiance is distinctly international, attracting the rich and famous from around the world, with a strong Cuban influence in terms of local food and dialect.

The main drag is Ocean Drive, directly in front of the beach and lined with pastel-colored art deco buildings: hotels, trendy boutiques, sizzling nightspots, sidewalk restaurants, art galleries. Although the prime attraction is the people more than the beach, the beach itself does happen to be a nice one—a wide stretch of soft white sand and the blue, blue Atlantic Ocean. It's more a chair beach than a towel one, and they're rented up and down the beach for a minimal three dollars to five dollars a day.

Although many of the art deco hotels have been renovated and are quite luxurious, there are a fair number that have not been renovated but market themselves as trendy nonetheless. Look carefully at brochures and ask questions to make sure that the hotel you choose is "old-style" and not just plain "old."

Also keep at least half an eye on the streets rather than the stars when you're out and about. The action takes place on four main avenues, perfectly safe for strolling at most hours, but if you go too far in the wrong direction, you'll quickly get into some pretty seedy areas. Don't forget: The unique charm of South Beach is that it's tropical *urban.*

Monaco

LOCATION: Independent principality surrounded by southeast France; fifteen miles from Nice

HIGH SEASON: May–October LOW SEASON: November–April

CONTACT: Monaco Government Tourist Office, 565 Fifth Avenue, 23rd floor, New York, NY 10017; (800) 753-9696, (212) 286-3330; fax: (212) 286-9890 http://www.monaco.mc/usa

An elegant enclave between the Alps and the Mediterranean, Monaco is an independent principality tucked between the French Riviera to the west and the Italian Riviera to the east, and has been ruled by the Grimaldi family since the thirteenth century, embodied today in the person of Prince Rainier. So small that it would fit inside New York City's Central Park, the tiny principality of Monaco—only three miles long by one-half-mile wide—has been attracting the beautiful people since the railroad first made its way there in the late eighteenth century.

Then, as now, one of the main attractions was the ornate, baroque Casino of Monte-Carlo. Its outside provides almost as much a spectacle as the interior, as the Rolls-Royces, Ferraris, and Lamborghinis pull up to deliver bejeweled film stars, musicians, and high rollers from the world over. Unlike the often raucous atmosphere of American casinos, the Casino of Monte-Carlo maintains an atmosphere of refined elegance, even going as far as enforcing a strict dress code. It sports European-style games of chance, such as roulette and chemin de fer, although in a nod to tourists, American-style slot machines have been added. The Café de Paris and the Loews Monte-Carlo are the place for other American games, such as blackjack and craps.

The principality's hotels are among the finest on the Riviera, especially the Hotel de Paris and the Hotel Hermitage, both exquisite old-world hotels that still attract the royal and the rich.

Although one might think this capital of the Côte d'Azur would have great beaches, it doesn't. The majority of the beach area is rocky and rough, and downright inaccessible in most places, although beautiful to look at from atop the cliffs. There is, however, one public sand beach called Larvotto, near Le Meridien Beach Plaza, a short walk from the heart of Monte-Carlo. Le Meridien has its own private sand beach, as does the Monte-Carlo Beach Hotel. Monaco is a short drive from other

Côte d'Azur towns that do have beaches, such as Nice and Cap d'Antibes.

Acapulco

LOCATION: Southwest coast of Mexico
HIGH SEASON: December–March LOW SEASON: July–October
CONTACT: Mexican Government Tourism Office,
405 Park Avenue, Suite 1401, New York, NY 10022;
(800) 44-MEXICO, (212) 421-6655, (212) 838-2949;
fax: (212) 753-2874
http://mexico-travel.com

The oldest of Mexico's beach resorts, we can thank Acapulco for tourism innovations that have become standard throughout the world: all-night discos, swim-up pool bars, pyramid-shaped hotels, even parasailing. The city started attracting the jet set back in the sixties when the word still meant something and the rich and famous flocked to build their hillside villas and enjoy the sandy white beaches. Jack and Jackie honeymooned here; Liz got married here.

Then in the eighties, the resort queen's golden crown tarnished. The crowds didn't diminish but they took on a different quality, the beaches were dirty, the sight of beggars became more familiar than movie stars. In the past several years, though, the city has taken to re-creating itself, spending millions to clean up and recapture its glitter and glamour. The Acapulco of today might not be quite what it was in its heyday, but it's certainly back on track, again attracting a beautiful crowd that wants to play hard at the beach all day and party hard all night long.

In addition to the million-dollar mansions that line the cliffs along the bay, Acapulco has more than sixteen thousand hotel rooms, mostly along the action-packed Costera Miguel Aleman, a glamorous strip that includes Condesa Beach and most of the city's fashionable restaurants, nightclubs, and hotels along the bay, and a newer area called Acapulco Diamante, where a luxury resort area is being developed from the southern tip of Puerto Marques down to Revolcadero Beach.

All the water sports you could ever want are available directly in front of the hotels, including the parasailing for which the city is so well known. For snorkeling the favorite is Roqueta Island, but the area also attracts numerous boats so you do have to pay attention. For diving instruction, Caleta Beach is the place, while the pounding surf of Revolcadero Beach is the favorite location for experienced surfers. To get away from it all, try the primitive, out-of-the-way beach at Barra Vieja or water-skiing at the Coyuca or Tres Palos fresh water lagoons. Don't miss the fabulous sunsets at Pie de la Cuesta beach and the extraordinary cliff divers who plunge hundreds of feet into the crashing Pacific Ocean several times a day at La Quebrada.

East Hampton

LOCATION: Long Island
HIGH SEASON: July–August LOW SEASON: November–April
CONTACT: East Hampton Chamber of Commerce, 79A Main Street, East Hampton, NY 11937; (516) 324-0362; fax: (516) 329-1642
http://www.peconic.net/community/eh-chamber

At first glance, East Hampton isn't at all the ritzy beach resort that one might expect: no fancy high-rise hotels, no glittering nightclubs, no crowds thronging around a photo shoot. This is, after all, where the celebs come to get away from it all. To varying degrees, the five main areas of East Hampton—Wainscott, East Hampton Village, Springs, Amagansett, and Montauk—all combine the well-heeled with the down-to-earth, the sophisticated with the quaint, the modern with the rustic.

East Hampton is probably the best-known of the

communities, a historic village with little modern clutter, closely followed by Amagansett, another historical town although there are more marks of modern tourism here.

Although you might easily see the stars out and about attending to regular business during the day—walking dogs, shopping, in-line skating—it's less likely you'll run into them at night unless you already know the right people yourself. Nightlife around here revolves around some very expensive restaurants and an exclusive round of parties and social events.

There are numerous beaches in the area, most white, sandy, and free of the honky-tonk atmosphere that comes with beach hotels and boardwalks. In fact, many of the beaches maintain an aura of exclusivity by requiring parking stickers (for residents only). There is, however, public parking for a daily fee at Main Beach, East Hampton and Atlantic Avenue, Amagansett, for those without a parking sticker. To really get away from it all, consider Cedar Point County Park, a quiet spot on a point that juts into Gardiner's Bay. The historic Cedar Point Lighthouse stood on an island two hundred yards from shore when it was built in 1860, but the hurricane of 1938 transformed the shoreline, shifting sands to create a narrow, walkable strip that now connects the lighthouse with the mainland.

Although summer is high season, the relatively new Hamptons International Film Festival, which draws top-line talent such as Steven Spielberg, Martin Scorsese, Isabella Rosselini, and Anjelica Huston, takes place in October.

Saint-Tropez

LOCATION: Southeast coast of France
HIGH SEASON: July–August LOW SEASON: October
CONTACT: French Government Tourist Office,

444 Madison Avenue, 16th floor, New York, NY 10022;
(900) 990-0040 ($.50/minute); fax: (212) 838-7855
http://www.francetourism.com

Tourists have been flocking to Saint-Tropez since Guy de Maupassant wrote about the serenity and stunning colors of the sleepy little port town in the late nineteenth century. But it wasn't until Brigitte Bardot hit town in the late 1950s with director Roger Vadim that all the world took note. Even though the town fell out of favor with the high-end international crowd in the eighties, Bardot still owns a villa there and the nineties have seen the influx of numerous other celebrities, including regulars like Liza Minnelli, Sylvester Stallone, and Cher.

Although there are some rocky public beaches in town, the place to acquire that much-touted Saint-Tropez tan is Pampelonne, a sandy crescent a couple of miles south of the port where beach clubs offer admission to a privileged world for the price of just a few dollars. On the beach and off, the right clothing is essential in this town (although on these beaches, less is definitely more), and the narrow medieval streets of town provide more than ample opportunity for trendy boutique shopping if you find yourself lacking.

Not surprisingly, hotels come in on the high end, ranging from the Hotel Byblos, a sort of fantasyland that imitates a quaint Provencale village (where rooms can reach as high as one thousand dollars a night in the high season), to the Château de la Messardiere, built around a restored nineteenth-century chateau. Restaurants, too, are not for the faint of heart when it comes to pricing—a dinner for two can easily run a couple of hundred dollars.

On the other hand, a very real working population still inhabits parts of Saint-Tropez. Down in the harbor, local fisherfolk still moor their boats next to the yachts, and just a few minutes out of town are rural farms, vineyards, and medieval villages where prices are more reasonable.

Estoril

LOCATION: Central west coast of Portugal
HIGH SEASON: July–August LOW SEASON: December–March
CONTACT: Portuguese National Tourist Office, 590 Fifth Avenue, New York, NY 10036; (800) PORTUGAL, (212) 354-4403; fax: (212) 764-6137
http://www.portugal.org

Although Estoril might not be as well known among Americans as some other European beach resorts, it's been a favorite for deposed European royalty, a playground for the wealthy, and a hotbed of international intrigue since World War II, when many fled to the neutral Portugal to escape the Nazis. It's the main resort along the twenty-mile Costa do Sol, right outside of Lisbon, and its famous residents have led to the area's second nickname: Costa dos Reis, or the Coast of Kings, although renowned inhabitants are just as likely to include counts, princesses, barons, and pretenders to the thrones of numerous countries.

The main beach, Tamiriz Beach, is wide, sandy, and beautiful, peopled with some of the most elegant high society of all Europe lounging under brightly striped beach umbrellas. Most beachgoers here choose to sun themselves rather than swim, as the ocean itself hasn't fared as well as the beach: The Atlantic Ocean around here is highly polluted, leading most swimmers to opt for hotel pools instead.

At night, the main attraction is the Casino of Estoril, which offers floor shows and dancing as well as gaming. At the tip of the town's centerpiece square, the Parque Estorial, the casino is just a few steps from the town's most famous hotel, the Palacio. Built in the 1930s, the

Palacio hosted most of the transient royalty who came to the area, while those who chose to make Estoril their new home usually opted to build hillside villas.

More modern hotels and high-rise apartments line the beach, extending as far as Cascais, a former fishing village four miles west that has catapulted into the international resort scene as well. In the harbor, the colorful boats of local fisherfolk vie for space with visiting yachts, while the pretty little downtown area sports expensive boutiques along its cobblestoned streets. The town has hotels in all categories, with one of the most expensive and best known being the Albatroz, a villa on a rock ledge above the ocean that has hosted the likes of Cary Grant, Prince Rainier and Princess Grace, and Claudette Colbert.

Malibu

LOCATION: Southern California; sixteen miles north of the Los Angeles Airport
HIGH SEASON: June–August LOW SEASON: October–March
CONTACT: Malibu Area Chamber of Commerce, 23805 Stuart Ranch Road, Suite 100, Malibu, CA 90265; (310) 456-9025; fax: (310) 456-0195
http://www.malibu.org

The beauty of Malibu is that you can watch for celebrities while exploring hidden coves and tide pools or playing volleyball and riding world-class waves. Known as Malibu Colony in the 1930s when the first lots were offered for lease to movie celebrities, today famous residents include Ingrid Bergman, Demi Moore, Madonna, Elle MacPherson, Brad Pitt, Keanu Reeves, Jim Carrey, and Antonio Banderas. The popular TV show *Baywatch* proved the astonishing appeal of this southern California beach, or maybe the estimated 2.4 billion people in over 120 countries are just watching the faux-Malibu lifeguards in their swimwear stretched to the bursting point. Despite Malibu's influential residents, California law protects public access to beaches. Yet the access points are sometimes hidden in the Malibu residential areas, where a narrow row of spectacular mansions cuts into the steep hillside below the Pacific Coast Highway. Look for small, brown signs with white lettering, and stay within the public boundary on the beach, below the mean high-tide line. Visitors should take a hint from "Bay Watch" and always swim near an on-duty lifeguard; rip currents are a dangerous hazard along this coastline.

Flawless bodies can be found up and down the coast, but the best socializing is found at Surfrider Beach next to the Malibu pier where you have to compete with serious surfers for the near-perfect waves. Zuma (never say "Zuma Beach") has strong surf suitable for bodysurfing, and the teens from Malibu High School tend to hang out there because it's near their school. If you're looking for a party, head for MTV's Malibu Beach House.

Accommodations are scarce in Malibu, with only a handful of beachside inns and roadside motels, so if you want to go economy-class, make plans to sleep in nearby Santa Monica. But you can get exceptionally fine dining in Malibu, from sushi to seafood, from Thai to French. Sometimes you might even catch a glimpse of Cindy Crawford or Arnold Schwarzenegger sitting at a nearby table.

Capri

LOCATION: Island in the Bay of Naples, off the coast of Naples, Italy
HIGH SEASON: May–September LOW SEASON: October–April
CONTACT: Italian Government Tourist Board, Rockefeller Center, 630 Fifth Avenue, New York, NY 10111; (212) 245-4822; fax: (212) 586-9249

A little island in the Bay of Naples, Capri has been

attracting the rich and famous since Roman times when Augustus retreated here to relax and Tiberius was so enchanted with the island's spectacular beauty that he actually moved the Imperial capital here. In this century, it's been the fabled hangout of the well-heeled for decades, most notably European movie stars who've built villas that perch precariously along the cliffsides and a number of artists and writers who come for its serene beauty. Today, despite the numerous tourists who daytrip from Naples and Sorrento, the island still has an air of the well-to-do, a certain panache that can be seen in everything from the chic inhabitants to the upscale boutiques to several fine hotels.

While you can easily get ripped off in the main tourist areas, hotels and restaurants actually tend to be cheaper than on mainland Italy. The finest hotels along the lower level of Capri town have seaside views (although none are beachside), while those up in the hilltop Anacapri offer even more stunning vistas of the cliffsides and bay below. Capri is also doable for those on a budget, with numerous charming and quite inexpensive pensiones. Although the island is, obviously, surrounded by water, most of the coast is not actual beach. For sunning and swimming, head to Marina Picola, where houses and restaurants front the pebble beach. During high season, it's hard to get a spot, but it's pleasantly quiet during off season.

A must-see on any trip to Capri is the Blue Grotto, where a quirk of the sunlight produces an exquisite blue color. Granted, the boat trips are extremely touristy—the guides have this stuff down pat and can get you in and out in minutes when it's busy—but the experience is still well worth it. If you take a boat trip around the island, you'll also have the chance to see lesser known green, yellow, pink, and white grottoes, not quite as spectacular as the blue one, but still interesting.

From Capri, it's only about half an hour on hydrofoil to the town of Naples, known for its spaghetti and beautiful women, among other attractions. About fourteen miles inland from Naples is Pompeii, preserved forever under the volcanic ash that exploded out of Mount Vesuvius some two thousand years ago.

Palm Beach

LOCATION: Southeast Florida

HIGH SEASON: November–March LOW SEASON: May–September

CONTACT: Palm Beach County Convention and Visitors Bureau, 1555 Palm Beach Lakes Boulevard, Suite 204, West Palm Beach, FL 33401; (800) 833-5733, (561) 471-3995; fax: (561) 471-3990 http://www.palmbeachfl.com

If a stroll down Palm Beach's Worth Avenue, one of the most renowned—and expensive—shopping streets in North America, doesn't make you at least secretly yearn to don a broad-rimmed hat and some fancy white gloves, nothing will. Although Palm Beach wasn't actually developed until Standard Oil magnate Henry Flagler built Whitehall in 1901 as a gift to his wife and a concrete expression of his vision of a state completely accessible by railroad, the feel here is decidedly old money. Think Kennedy compound (still called that even though the Kennedys don't own it anymore). Think chauffeured limousines. Think Chanel, Armani, Gucci, and Tiffany—without even having to look at your credit card balance first.

Yes, it's a whole different world here. Plush, posh, and powerful, Palm Beach still reigns as a queen of old-style gentility, even though it has made some concessions to the present. You'll probably be greeted affably even if you're in jeans now—at least until the shopkeepers get a chance to check out your jewelry, manicure, and handbag to determine if you're a new-style paying shopper or a run-of-the-mill window-shopper.

Of course, the beaches are well-maintained here, but in truth, they're rather narrow and not the best in the area. Unless you're staying at a hotel like the exclusive Breakers, which has its own private beach, also be prepared for gawkers strolling along the city-owned promenade that runs from Gulf Stream Road at the beach's northern boundary to Royal Palm Way at the south. On the other hand, if you're just in for the day yourself, the promenade provides a great way to experience the ocean sounds and smells without dealing with sand in your shoes. A low stone wall separates the promenade from the beach proper, opening occasionally for a few steps that lead down to the beach. And though the beach is free, the parking isn't—it's metered in increments of fifteen minutes, so have a hefty supply of quarters on hand and expect to jump up frequently to feed the little tyrants.

There are numerous other beaches within easy driving distance, most of which also require either parking or entry fees. Some of the best in the area include Boca Raton's Red Reef Park for snorkelers, Boca's South Beach Park for dune-lovers, and Lake Worth Municipal Beach and Barton Park for surfers, to name just a few.

Martha's Vineyard

LOCATION: Island off the coast of Cape Cod, Massachusetts
HIGH SEASON: July–August LOW SEASON: November–December
CONTACT: Martha's Vineyard Chamber of Commerce, Inc.,
P.O. Box 1698, Beach Road, Vineyard Haven, MA 02568;
(508) 693-0085; fax: (508) 693-7589
http://www.mvy.com

The best way to get a feel for the real Martha's Vineyard

is to rent a house here. (Okay, the best way is to buy a place where you can call Carly Simon, Walter Cronkite, or Beverly Sills neighbor in addition to the possibilities of temporary residents along the lines of President Clinton and his family.) The reason is simple: Many of the best beaches on the island are restricted to residents and summer visitors staying in the towns where the beaches are located. Staying a while also gives you a chance to delve into the private life of the island, the glamour of which lies more in its unpretentious acceptance of celebrities than fauning voyeurism.

The biggest of the vacation islands off the New England coast, Martha's Vineyard roughly separates into east and west, with Edgartown on the east side having the most inns, restaurants, and upscale shops, as well as yachts sailing into its harbor and the mansions of sea captains from the island's whaling days lining its streets. It also offers the most popular island beaches (all accessible to the public), most notably Katama Beach, also called South Beach, a three-mile stretch of barrier beach with the strong Atlantic surf on one side and a salt pond on the other. To escape the crowds (thousands strong on summer weekends), just take a ferry to Chappaquiddick, where East Beach and its magnificent dunes are located right by the Dike Bridge (yes, *that* bridge) and a remote land of untouched wilderness.

Other popular beaches that are accessible to the public include Joseph Sylvia State Beach, two miles of clear, mild beach between Edgartown and Oak Bluffs that is especially popular with families; Lobsterville Beach, two miles of beautiful, narrow Vineyard Sound beach and dunes that includes a seagull nesting area and is a favorite fishing spot (open to all but no parking); and Menemsha Public Beach, also on the sound, next to the harbor, with bright clear waters and great sunsets.

"Up island" includes the more rural, remote parts of the island, and some great residents-only beaches, including Lambert's Cove Beach, considered by many to have the finest sand and clearest water on the North Shore (West Tisbury), Squibnocket Beach for surfing (Chilmark), and Lucy Vincent Beach, with a strong surf and clay bluffs (Chilmark).

10

One of a Kind

The Best Beaches for Unique Opportunities

The Dead Sea

LOCATION: Southeast Israel
HIGH SEASON: September–May LOW SEASON: June–August
CONTACT: Israel Government Tourist Office, 800 Second Avenue, New York, NY 10017; (888) 77 ISRAEL, (212) 499-5660; fax: (212) 499-5665
http:///www.goisrael.com

A blue-green lake surrounded by dramatic rocky deserts, the Dead Sea is both the lowest point on the face of the earth—more than thirteen hundred feet below sea level—and the saltiest body of water anywhere, with a 30 percent concentration of salt and minerals. Because of that, virtually nothing can live in it—hence the name—and the water is incredibly buoyant. You can't swim in this sea, but even nonswimmers can float easily. Almost frighteningly effortlessly, in fact, until you get used to it: Just squat down and the water itself propels your legs up and out so you're resting on your back. Don't forget to bring a prop in with you for the standard photo op—stretched out on your back, reading the newspaper!

A warning, though: Because the water does have so many minerals, it feels different from regular lake or even ocean water, almost oily. And if you have any open sores, the salt in the water can produce a burning sensation. All told, it takes some getting used to.

Stretching forty-seven miles from top to bottom, the area has been known for thousands of years as a site for rejuvenation and healing. It's not just the minerals in the water, but also the thermal springs and therapeutic black mud. Even the very air has more oxygen and bromine than in other places, resulting in a relaxed state especially good for breathing and almost guaranteeing a suntan instead of a sunburn. Archeologists have even discovered what they believe to be an ancient cosmetics factory with evidence that it served Cleopatra.

For decades, the area was visited chiefly for its healing and therapeutic effects on skin, breathing, and joint disorders, but in recent years, it's become more of a tourist site in its own right. Although there's no real urban center, there are some twenty-two hundred hotel rooms now, expected to increase to about four thousand by the year 2000. Until recently, most were in bungalows and tourist-class hotels, but the opening of the Hyatt Regency Dead Sea Resort Spa in 1996 paved the way for other upscale hotels and entertainment options.

The area is also rich in historic treasures: Qumran, where the Dead Sea Scrolls were discovered; Masada, where Jewish zealots held off Roman troops for years before committing mass suicide; and Mount Sodom in the south, where the numerous eerie salt pillars that line it encourage visitors to try to guess which one might be the wife of the Old Testament Lot.

Assateague Island

LOCATION: Part in Worcester County, Maryland; part in Accomack County, Virginia
HIGH SEASON: Mid-June–Labor Day
LOW SEASON: December–March
CONTACT: Assateague Island National Seashore, 7206 National Seashore Lane, Berlin, MD 21811; (410) 641-1441

While it might have been common for wild horses and people to share living space hundreds of years ago, one of the few places it happens now is at Assateague, a windswept barrier island that straddles Maryland and Virginia. No one's really sure how the wild horses, called "ponies" by the locals, got there, but one myth holds that a Spanish galleon sank in the area and the horses swam to shore. No matter what their origin, there they remain. Most of the time, at least. The last Wednesday and Thursday of July is the pony pen and swim, when excess horses are rounded up to go to Chincoteague, where they are auctioned off.

Except during the pen and swim, you won't see masses of horses galloping down the beach together. More likely, you'll see a few gathered in a group, most often at dusk and during the evenings. If you're camping, you might even find a couple right outside your tent, searching through your gear for some good munchies. Do follow the warnings not to feed the horses (though I certainly wouldn't tell one to stop if it's already found something it likes), and remember that they are wild: They've been known to kick and bite when people get too close.

The only way to actually spend the night on Assateague Island is camping. Although there are several facilities within walking distance of the beach, they fill up just like hotel rooms, so either reserve ahead of time (call the National Seashore at 800-365-2267 or Assateague State Park for weekly rentals at 410-641-2120) or get there early in the day. If you prefer a bed to a sleeping bag, the north entrance to Assateague is only eight miles south of Ocean City, Maryland, where there are numerous beachside hotels and motels and a lively boardwalk (see chapter 1), and the south entrance is a mere two miles from Chincoteague, where there are also hotels and motels.

For swimming, there are white-sand beaches at either end of the island. Another fifteen miles of beach is accessible to four-wheel-drive vehicles, and nineteen miles have been preserved as wild shoreland for hikers and beachcombers to experience the outdoors in the same way as the original Indian inhabitants and the first European explorers.

Santorini

LOCATION: Southernmost island in the Cyclades, Greece
HIGH SEASON: May–September LOW SEASON: October–April
CONTACT: Greece National Tourist Office, 645 Fifth Avenue, New York, NY 10022; (212) 421-5777; fax: (212) 826-6940 http:///www.compulink.gr/tourism

While Santorini is certainly not the only island ever formed or disturbed by volcanic activity, it is one of the very few sites that scholars seriously consider as a possible origin of Plato's legend of the lost continent Atlantis. That a great volcanic eruption took place around 1500 B.C. (creating tidal waves huge enough to destroy the palace of Knossos on Crete) is beyond doubt: The island's craggy high cliffs, the walls of the ancient volcano, soar nine hundred feet above sea level and wrap around a bay, in the center of which a volcanic crater plunges twelve hundred feet.

Santorini is actually several islands, the newest of which appeared as recently as 1772 and is a now-dormant volcano that expanded with each of its explosions, the most recent in 1956. The main town is called Thíra, the ancient name of the island; today the whole island is often referred to as Thíra. Getting to the town is in itself an experience: It perches atop the rugged black lava cliffs, and the only options for reaching it are to climb the more than eight hundred slippery steps that lead from the bay to the town, take a cable car, or pay a rather exorbitant fee for an escorted donkey ride to the top (for an additional fee, you can have the photos that prove you made the journey).

In contrast to the sheer cliffs on the west side of the island, the east side features black-sand and pebble beaches, a constant reminder of the power of the volcano. Kamari, a relatively modern town facing the beach, is the most popular beach site for tourists, while Monolithos and Perissa are less crowded. Near Perissa is Ancient Thíra, with ruins dating as far back as the ninth century B.C. The ruins at Akrotiri are the remains of the Minoan city that was destroyed by the cataclysmic eruption in 1500 B.C.; nearby, red lava cliffs soar over the black sandy beach also called Akrotiri.

Atlantic City

LOCATION: East coast of southern New Jersey
HIGH SEASON: June–September LOW SEASON: December–February
CONTACT: Atlantic City Convention and Visitors Bureau,
2314 Pacific Avenue, Atlantic City, NJ 08401; (609) 449-7100,
(800) BOARDWK; fax: (609) 345-3685
http:///www.atlanticcitynj.com

Sure, lots of other beaches have casinos. But nowhere else do they line up like in Atlantic City, where you can easily walk from one to another to yet another—fourteen at present with more in the works. A premier beach resort from the end of the last century right through the middle of this century, Atlantic City bucked the odds and reinvented itself in 1977 when gambling was legalized there. The casinos are the center of action night and day, both for the twenty-four-hour gaming possibilities and a roster of star-studded live entertainment which rivals that of Las Vegas.

Most of the casinos line the famous four-mile Boardwalk, the first ever constructed, in 1870. Walking the boards is still a highlight, with stops at a variety of shops that range from top-of-the-line boutiques to tacky-souvenir vendors; the famous Steel Pier, along with a host of other piers that feature rides and entertainment; and food outlets galore: pizza, soft ice cream, and the city's renowned salt water taffy, to name just a few possibilities. And if you walk too far in one direction, not to worry: The rolling chairs instituted over a century ago still make their way up and down the Boardwalk.

In and out of the casinos, fine dining abounds, at old favorites such as the Knife and Fork Inn, where the movie *Atlantic City* was filmed, and the Renault Winery, the oldest in the country, or at newcomers such as Hard Rock Café, All-Star Café, and Planet Hollywood.

The beach itself is one of the few remaining free beaches in New Jersey—in most places a wide expanse of hard-packed sand where sun-worshippers mingle with those who've just stepped out of the casinos for a breath of fresh air. The Atlantic City crowd is eclectic, to say the least, made up of teenagers who live in the city, families who spend summer weekends "down the shore," high-rollers in to take their chances, and Social Security grandmothers who've taken the bus in for the day.

Although there are already fourteen thousand hotel rooms in the city and another nine thousand in the works, getting a room without a reservation can be tricky, especially at the casinos, so it's best to plan in advance. Another caveat: Think twice before leaving the main drag along the Boardwalk; although the city has already spent billions of dollars on revitalization, many parts outside of the tourist areas are still more than a little dicey.

Punalu'u

LOCATION: Southeast coast of Big Island of Hawaii, Hawaii
HIGH SEASON: December–February, June–August
LOW SEASON: March–May, September–November
CONTACT: Hawaii Visitors and Convention Bureau,
180 Montgomery Street, Suite 2360, San Francisco, CA 94104;
(800) 353-5846, (415) 248-3800; fax: (415) 248-3808
http://www.gohawaii.com

The youngest of the Hawaiian Islands, the Big Island of Hawaii is not only the largest but is still growing an average of forty-two acres a year as the Kilauea Volcano continues to explode. While the beaches that line the island's Kohala Coast on the north have become renowned both for their palm-fringed white sand and the super-luxury resorts that have sprung up in the area, they're nothing compared to the black sand along the long curving beach of Punalu'u.

Black-sand beaches can be formed only when the molten lava of a volcano hits the cooler ocean water and turns into millions of black granules that wash back to the shore. They usually come and go with new flows of lava or are quickly eroded. So far, though, the beach at Punalu'u has proven to be an exception, with the black sand continuing to wash back in to re-form a beach.

Although the view along the curving crescent is gorgeous—the turquoise bay contrasting with the jet-black sand and coconut palms in the background—the current is powerful and sometimes dangerous here. The safest part is the north end, where swimmers, snorkelers, and surfers congregate. Parts of Punalu'u also have green sand, though not as much as at the aptly named Green Sand Beach at the southern tip of the island, where the olive-green granules were produced by crushed olivine mineral deposits in the lava.

Accommodations in the area are extremely limited—some bed-and-breakfasts and condos, but camping is permitted on the meadows behind the beach. Kailua-Kona, about sixty miles away on the west coast, and Hilo, approximately 60 miles to the north on the eastern shore, provide the most plentiful accommodations options. To get from Hilo to Punalu'u, you drive right through Hawaii Volcanoes National Park—well worth exploring in its own right. The volcano Kilauea still erupts there, and the thousands of acres of the park are ripe with lava tubes, fern forests, lunar landscapes, and misty steaming vents. The caldera of Kilauea is said to be the home of the great fire goddess Pele.

Galápagos Islands

LOCATION: Islands six hundred miles off the coast of Ecuador in the Pacific Ocean
HIGH SEASON: July–September, November–January
LOW SEASON: October, February–June
CONTACT: Ecuador Consulate, 800 Second Avenue, Suite 600, New York, NY 10017; (212) 808-0170; fax: (212) 808-0188

Traveling to the Galápagos Islands now isn't all that different than when Charles Darwin went there nearly two centuries ago. Sure, there are a few more people, but many of the islands are still uninhabited—by people, that is. Fortunately, they're still home to fun-loving sea lions, prehistoric-looking iguanas, the only penguins that live in a tropical zone, giant tortoises, and the little finches that ultimately were the inspiration for Darwin's *On the Origin of the Species,* which in turn led to the theory of natural selection and the still-controversial theory of the evolution of humans.

Although no one goes to the islands simply to lie on the beach, the beaches are an added bonus to the incredible experience of seeing this unique ecosystem. You can stay in a range of hotels (although nothing that remotely resembles "luxury") in Puerto Ayora, the main town on Isla Santa Cruz, and take daytrips or short overnights from there, but the most common way to see the islands is on what are very loosely called "cruise ships." If your image of a cruise runs to hundreds of people, endless food, nonstop entertainment, and dressing up, forget it. The entertainment on these cruises is the islands, most are limited to under sixty passengers, and the food is, well, edible for the most part.

But that's okay because most of the day you'll spend exploring the islands, with the ships doing their traveling during the night. Physically, these trips are demanding—you get up early, frequently have to jump out of a small boat and wade through the ocean to get to an island, and can spend hours hiking around. If you don't have the physical stamina or a real interest, don't go. Already the volume of tourists has disturbed the fragile environment, so leave it for those who really do want to experience it.

Even though tourism has increased somewhat, the wildlife is still friendly, basically because the creatures don't *know* to be afraid of humans. Although the exact islands that you'll visit vary by ship, most include Isla Santa Cruz, site of Charles Darwin Research Station and the giant tortoises; Isla Mosquera, where you can lie on the tiny sandy beach with the sea lions or frolic with them in the water; Isla San Salvador, where huge marine iguanas bask in the sunlight along the long, flat black-lava beach; and Isla Bartolomé, where just off the small, sandy beach you can snorkel and swim with the Galapagos penguins, marine turtles, and tropical fish.

Easter Island

LOCATION: Southeastern Pacific Ocean

HIGH SEASON: December–February LOW SEASON: July–August

CONTACT: There is no Chile Tourism Office in the United States, but the national airline Lan Chile Airlines can supply country information: Lan Chile Airlines, 630 Fifth Avenue, Suite 809, New York, NY 10111; (800) 735-5526, (212) 582-3250; fax: (212) 582-6863

Called the most remote island in the world, the Chilean dependency of Easter Island rises mysteriously in the Pacific Ocean, two thousand miles from Chile, two thousand miles from Tahiti, alone, remote, and inexplicable. No one knows exactly who made the gigantic statues that litter the island, or why. Or why they ceased to create them. Speculation abounds, of course, but at this point, that's all it is. The huge monoliths of humans, called *moai* and numbering around six hundred, are mostly about twelve feet tall, but the largest rises as high as thirty-seven feet. They've all been toppled from their bases, apparently intentionally, although again the reason is a question mark. In addition to the statues, the islanders possessed the Rongorongo script, the only written language in Oceania and still undeciphered, as well as petroglyphs (rock carvings) and colorful cave paintings of birds in flight, all of which only lead to more mystery.

Today the island is locally called Rapa Nui, as are the people and the language. Virtually all of the some three thousand inhabitants live in Hangaroa, on the west coast, and the adjoining settlement Mataveri. The interior of the island consists of about eighty volcanic cones of different sizes and rocky plains, with volcanic tubes that have formed an extensive system of caves—mostly unexplored in modern times, so if you do go spelunking, you never quite know what you'll come across.

The coastline is rugged, with high black cliffs and only a few white-sand beaches, the most popular being Anakena, opposite Hangaroa Village. Not only is it a beautiful beach fronting gorgeous open turquoise waters, but you can swim in the shadow of six *moai* and the tomb of Thor Heyerdahl, one of the island's early explorers. According to tradition, the beach is also the site of the landing of the mythical founder of Rapa Nui, Hotu Matu'a, or "Great Parent."

You can explore the rest of the island in tours that run as quickly as half a day to as leisurely as a full week depending on your level of interest. Plan on a good three days of sightseeing to adequately cover the basics, including Rano Raraku, where the *moai* were carved and there is one especially unusual one of a kneeling man with a goatee; Ahu Akahanga, right below Rano Raraku, where fifteen restored *moai* stand; and the Orongo crater near the ceremonial village of Orongo, where "birdman" competitions were held and petroglyphs abound.

Amenities on the island are very basic, with accommodations in about ten hotels and several guest houses, where you can still get a room for about fifteen dollars a night.

Komodo Island

LOCATION: Island of Indonesia, east of Bali
HIGH SEASON: June–August LOW SEASON: December–March
CONTACT: Indonesia Tourist Promotion Office,
3457 Wilshire Boulevard, Los Angeles, CA 90010;
(213) 387-8309; fax: (213) 380-4876

What's that? There's no such thing as dragons? Well, think again. There really are about three thousand Komodo dragons living on Komodo Island (the dragons came first, then the island name), between the islands of Sumbawa and Flores near Bali.

The dragons are the last descendants of carnivorous dinosaurs and are thought to have been extinct everywhere else since the Jurassic age. Although they were probably always known in Indonesia (in fact, Indonesians exiled outcasts to the island with the idea that they wouldn't be able to survive long), no one else in modern times knew about them until World War I when a pilot crashed into the waters near the island and later reported tales of giant reptiles on the island. No one believed him, but later explorations confirmed that the island really is home to prehistoric-looking carnivorous monsters that typically grow up to ten feet long and can weigh as much as three hundred pounds.

No, Komodo Island is not your typical beach vacation. It's only for the hardy (climbing around the island can be tough) and, frankly, the brave. Tall tales abound, but the truth is there have been at least some cases where the dragons have eaten humans. The bacteria in their saliva is also enough to kill a person from a bite alone. If, however, you have an interest in bizarre natural phenomena, it doesn't get much stranger than these creatures.

To explore the island, you *must* hire an official guide, who will take you to the places the dragons are known to congregate and, more important, make sure you don't go where you shouldn't. There used to be prearranged feedings for tourists (live goats), but that stopped a few years ago—one more reason not to wander through the underbrush alone and possibly make yourself lunch.

Accommodations on the island are at the official camp, Loh Liang, which fronts on a beach. The water right off the shore has sharp coral, so you do need to be careful swimming, but snorkeling is good (you also need to keep your eyes open—they say the dragons can swim, too). Between Komodo Island and the nearby island of Flores is some great diving and snorkeling, with the chance to see vibrant soft corals, exotic butterfly fish, huge tuna, and thousands of colorful tropical fish.

Playas del Este

LOCATION: Northwest coast of Cuba, just east of Havana
HIGH SEASON: November–March, July–August
LOW SEASON: April–June, September–October
CONTACT: There is no Cuban embassy or tourism office in the United States. For information, contact either the Cuban Interests Section, 2630 Sixteenth St. N.W., Washington, DC 20009; (202) 797-8518; or the Canadian office of the Cuba Tourist Board, 55 Queen Street E., Suite 705, Toronto, Ontario M5C 1R5; (416) 362-0700; fax: (416) 362-6799

What exactly is so special about a strip of resort beaches on the outskirts of a city? A lot, when the city is Havana. Yes, it is still illegal for Americans to go to Cuba (actually, it's illegal for most Americans to spend money in Cuba, which amounts to pretty much the same thing, with some exceptions). But that rule comes from the U.S. side, not the Cubans: They're quite happy to take our money, thank you very much. And take it they do—Americans are flocking to Havana, mostly business-people paving the way for an anticipated relaxing of the old rules, journalists (even JFK Jr. went recently to interview dad's old nemesis Fidel Castro), and young men who can't resist the kick of traveling to one of the few countries in the world forbidden to U.S. citizens.

Just getting there is half the adventure because there are no direct flights from the United States. So, in James Bond style, you go to either the Bahamas, Mexico, Jamaica, or Canada and from there to Cuba. The Cubans know, but just make sure they don't stamp your passport (how would you explain *that* coming back through Customs?).

Although there are several beach resorts throughout the country (catering mostly to Canadians and Europeans who never broke off ties with Cuba), Havana is *the* place to experience Cuba: to walk in the footsteps of Papa Hemingway, the Rat Pack, and Meyer Lansky; to smoke what are arguably the best cigars in the world; to make contacts of whatever kind you're interested in with Cubans who are hungry for news and information about the United States.

It's easy to combine a beach vacation with the big-city experience in Playas del Este, the run of beaches off the Straits of Florida that starts less than ten miles from city center at the palm-fringed Bacuranao and continues for another five miles through Tarará, El Mégano, Santa Maria del Mar, and Boca Ciega to the small town of Guanabo. By the time you reach Guanabo, you're pretty much out of the international tourist area, so the rates are considerably cheaper and you can hang with real Cubans if you want to. If you prefer a beach resort atmosphere, most of the dozen or so that line the beach are in Santa Maria del Mar.

Lipari

LOCATION: One of seven Aeolian Islands off the coast of Sicily, Italy
HIGH SEASON: January–March, July–August
LOW SEASON: April–June, September–December
CONTACT: Italian Government Tourist Board, Rockefeller Center, 630 Fifth Avenue, New York, NY 10111; (212) 245-4822; fax: (212) 586-9249

One of the Aeolian Islands (sometimes called the Lipari Islands), Lipari is popular among Italians and other Europeans but hasn't really caught on yet with Americans. One can only imagine it's because most of us have never heard of these islands—because once you know about them, they offer so many unusual features that they're hard to resist. One of the top lures is the pumice beach of Lipari. That's right—a soft white powdery beach with chunks of pumice spewed from the mouth of the island's volcano.

As the largest and most developed of the Aeolian Islands, Lipari offers several other interesting sightseeing features and a perfect base for excursions to the other islands. The main town on Lipari, also called Lipari (Confused yet? Lipari is the name of the chain, the island, and the town), is a bustling port divided into two sections: the café-lined Marina Corta, which is the hydrofoil port, and Marina Lunga, where the ferries dock. Between the two is Lipari's greatest human-made attraction: the seventeenth-century clifftop castle. It houses its archeological museum, a rare treasure trove of antiquities that date from Neolithic through Roman times, all found on the long-inhabited islands of the archipelago.

The nearby island Vulcano, named for the god of fire and metallurgy, also offers unusual beaches, most notably the black-sand beach with hot bubbling mud. Europeans don't seem to have a problem taking hot-mud baths there, viewing them as a free kind of beauty treatment, but do be prepared for the stench. Beyond the mud is an area where hot water bubbles to the surface just off the shore, creating a natural Jacuzzi that's ideal for washing off the smelly mud and relaxing. Once you're relaxed, you can take off for a hike to the top of the island's volcano—dormant but far from dead, with the steam and hiss to prove it—or to the top of the smaller Volcanello, a distinct island until it merged with Vulcano some two thousand years ago.

The third main tourist island is Stromboli (yes, like the food), where the world's most active volcano spews lava and hot ashes approximately every fifteen minutes. Hiking to peer over the edge of the crater is the main attraction here. You can do it on your own following the fairly well-marked hiking path, but it's advisable to go with a local guide who can recognize signs of unusual—and potentially dangerous—activity. The scene is most spectacular at night; camping by the crater for the pyrotechnics show is generally safe, but attempting the paths at night is not.

Appendixes

The Right Vacation

Even after reading about all these great beach vacations, you still might not be sure which one is right for you. Consider the following, and you might find your decision makes itself for you:

- *Budget* How much can you afford to pay? Although almost all the destinations in this book have accommodations in several price ranges, airfare is a lot less flexible. Also consider how much you might want to spend on restaurants, shopping, and other entertainment.
- *Time* How many days can you realistically be away? Will you be able to spend enough time to do everything you want to do? On the other hand, if you want to be away for two weeks, does the place you're considering have enough to keep you entertained the entire time?
- *Activity level* Do you want to lounge on the beach, sightsee, golf, do water sports? Make sure the area you're considering has facilities for everything you want to do.
- *Ambience* Luxurious or back-to-nature? American or international? Cosmopolitan or laid-back?
- *Accessibility* How long does it take to get there? For example, an island in the middle of the Pacific

that might take nearly two days to reach doesn't make much sense if all you have is one week. Can you get there directly or would you need to change planes? If you're driving, how much territory can you reasonably cover in a day?

- *Safety* Check government travel advisories to see if the area you're considering is deemed safe for travelers.

Working With a Travel Agent

First off, unless you know exactly where you want to go, how to get there, what hotel to stay at, and what to do while you're on your vacation, there's no reason *not* to work with a travel agent. Yes, they get commissions. No, that commission does not come out of your pocket. It's paid by the airlines, hotels, and tour operators to the travel agent, so your price will be exactly the same whether you work with an agent or not. In fact, it could quite easily be higher if you do it all on your own because travel agents have access to resources that aren't available to you (even with all the high-tech information sources around now).

The first step might be the most difficult: choosing a good travel agent. Start with referrals from friends, especially others who've gone to places similar to what you're looking for because travel agents often specialize in certain areas (cruising, corporate travel, adventures, and so on). As in any other profession, there are good travel agents and bad ones. And there will be some that are good, but who simply aren't a good fit for you. Whether you have a referral or walk in off the street, here are some things to consider:

- Is the agent/agency a member of the International Association of Travel Agents? While membership doesn't guarantee a good agent, it does indicate a certain level of professionalism.

- Does the agent have experience in the kind of travel you're interested in? For example, an agent can be great at booking exotic travel to the South Pacific but know nothing about Central America. (Tip: Watch what agents do when you first speak to them—can they come up with hotel names and information on the spot or do they need to check the computer or brochure to answer your most basic questions?)
- Does the agent question you about your preferences and habits before starting to make suggestions? You want a vacation that's good for you, not an off-the-shelf trip sold to anyone who walks in the door.
- Is the agent available to you during hours when it's convenient for you? Does the agency have a twenty-four-hour help line if you have a problem outside of regular business hours?
- When and in what form is payment necessary? What are refund policies in case of cancellation? Although it's unlikely that larger agencies will go out of business before your trip, a smaller agency always presents a certain financial risk—is your money protected in some way in case of closure? When possible, protect yourself by paying with a credit card rather than cash.

Planning Ahead

When I first started traveling, it was almost inevitable that I would forget to do or bring something important. No more, though. Now I have a checklist for things to do before I leave and things to make sure I pack. Your personal lists might be somewhat different, but start with these guidelines.

As soon as you know where you're going, get all the information on the following. You could end up in real trouble if you save these until the last minute:

- Travel documents you'll need—and make sure you have them (for travel outside of the United States, you usually need a passport, although some nearby places will accept an original birth certificate—with raised seal—and another form of official identification)
- Inoculations or other health precautions (malaria pills, for example, need to be started a couple of weeks before you actually go away)

In the week or two before you leave:

- Arrange with someone to bring in mail, water plants, and take care of children or animals. (Even if you don't need anyone to take care of anything for you, it's a good idea for at least one other person to have the key to your home in case of emergency while you're gone)

- If you're driving, plan your route; if you're leaving from an airport, decide how you will get there and ask someone to drive you if necessary
- Read up on the area so you have an idea what to expect when you get there
- Confirm all travel arrangements and make sure you have all necessary tickets, vouchers, etc.
- Leave an itinerary—complete with phone numbers—with at least one person at home
- A few days before you leave, consider ways to combat jet lag if you're traveling long distances. Despite the advice of experts, each person is different and handles it differently—you'll have to play around to find what works best for you, but consider taking melatonin, gradually trying to adjust your schedule to the new time zone before you leave home, or doing what seems to work best for me—not sleeping the night before you leave so that you're exhausted enough to sleep the entire time on the plane!

The day or two before:

- Make sure at least some lights are on a timer and decide if you're going to leave a radio or television on
- Buy anything you'll need that you don't already have (film, extra batteries, chewing gum for the plane)
- Eat, freeze, or throw away all perishable foods
- Stock up on some nonperishable food so you have something to eat the day you come home
- Set the VCR if there's something on television that you just can't miss while you're gone
- Confirm all plans one more time
- Pack
- Start to get excited!

Packing Tips

I've never understood the advice that most travel experts give when it comes to packing: Pack everything you want and then take out half. Why? Granted, if you're backpacking, you'll need to travel light. Same thing if you're doing an eight-cities-in-nine-days kind of tour and will never get the chance to unpack in any one place. But I'd always rather come home with a few things that I didn't wear than get caught short.

To figure what you'll need, simply calculate how many days and nights you'll be gone and think about what you expect to do during those times. Don't forget to factor in days when you might need several outfits; say you might do some sightseeing, go swimming, get dressed again for the afternoon, and then change again for the evening. One day, four outfits. When possible, pack tops and bottoms that can go with several other tops and bottoms. Do some mixing and matching and no one will realize you're repeating some of the same elements. Jackets, sweaters, ties, scarves, and necklaces all go a long way in transforming one outfit to another.

Now, all this is not to say you should get carried away. Chances are good that you'll end up carrying your bags at some point, if not all the time, so make sure you can comfortably lift them. And don't forget the shopping you might do while you're gone—either leave enough room for souvenirs or pack a little collapsible bag in your suitcase that you can use later if necessary.

Try to bring as few valuables with you as possible (especially costly jewelry—why set yourself up as a robbery target?), but if you do bring something expensive, such as a good camera, make sure you put it in a carry-on bag rather than in checked luggage. Your carry-on bag should also include anything irreplaceable or essential whether it has a high monetary value or not. Nobody else might want your glasses, medicine, or journal, but you could be lost without them.

If it's a long flight, in addition to reading materials, games, cards, and other things to keep you occupied, you might want to bring along supplies to do a quick touch-up: toothbrush and toothpaste, comb, hand cream (the air in planes is always dry), some cleanser or make-up. Not only will you feel better when you get off the flight, but if by some chance your baggage does get delayed en route, at least you'll have the essentials with you.

Finally, when I'm going to the beach, I always pack my bathing suit and suntan lotion in my carry-on. Even if everything else is lost on the way, what else do you really need?

Index